One Man's Horse

One Man's Horse

By MARGUERITE HENRY

Illustrated by Wesley Dennis
with famous paintings and
prints by selected artists

RAND McNALLY & COMPANY

CHICAGO · NEW YORK · SAN FRANCISCO

ACKNOWLEDGMENTS. All of the drawings in the story are by Wesley
Dennis and are used by permission of his sons. Grateful acknowledgment is
also made for the use of photographs on the pages indicated: Sidney M.
Morris and Jessie Simmons, pp. 77, 79, 95, 98, 99, 103; Philip A. Pines, p.
78; Janet Schwerdt Hack, pp. 81, 96, 104; Kenneth McQuarrie, p. 93; E.
Roland Harriman and Elbridge T. Gerry, p. 101; Donald P. Evans, p. 102;

and especially for history supplied by

Louise Carlin, descendant of Jonas Seely, Sr.; Maisie Conroy and Ann Roche,
Goshen Library and Historical Society; Jeanne Sharp, Reference Librarian,
genealogy section, Newburgh Library; Myrtle S. Edwards and Genevieve
Van Duzer, historians; Colleen Lofrese and Roberta B. Sutton, researchers;
Richard Banker of the Banker Farm, formerly the Jonas Seely place; Lester
Ford, *Harness Horse Magazine;* Milo Folley, *The Horseman and Fair
World;* Donald P. Evans, United States Trotting Association.

Book Design by MARIO PAGLIAI

Library of Congress Cataloging in Publication Data

Henry, Marguerite
  ONE MAN'S HORSE.

  Excerpts from the author's Born To Trot.
  SUMMARY: A fictionalized history of the horse credited
with fathering the standardbred line, accompanied by a pictorial
postlude of his ancestors and descendants.
    1. Hambletonian 10 (Horse)—Juvenile fiction.
2. Horses—Legends and stories. 3. Standardbred horse—
Juvenile literature. {1. Hambletonian 10 (Horse)—Fiction.
2. Horses—Fiction. 3. Standardbred horse} I. Title.
PZ10.3.H430 n 1977   {Fic}   77-10080
ISBN 0-528-82092-3
ISBN 0-528-80057-4 lib. bdg.

Contents

The Inside Story

When Dr. Mary Alice Jones, my former editor, first read the manuscript of *Born To Trot,* her comment was, "You have two distinct stories in this book. My suggestion would be to treat them separately... in two volumes instead of one."

But I held fast to the idea of interweaving young Gib White's story with that of a brawny, bearded Dutchman named Rysdyk and his trotting horse, Hambletonian. It seemed such an exciting challenge to write a story-within-a-story. I called the inner story *One Man's Horse* and hoped that through the eyes of a twentieth century boy I could tell the dramatic history of the founding father of the Standard Breed.

After the book was published *my* way, Dr. Jones never said "I told you so." But she couldn't help smiling at the steady trickle of letters asking me, "Where can I find a copy of *One Man's Horse?* Our library doesn't have it, and our bookstore never heard of it. Did you make it up?"

Just recently a very persistent letter-writer prodded me into rereading *One Man's Horse.* To my surprise I finally realized that Rysdyk's Hambletonian was a solid story in itself, a story based in history, and one that should be told uninterruptedly. It was almost as if I had never read the inner story before.

When I came to the end I studied the emblem—the word "finis" surrounded by laurel leaves with a horseshoe crest—and my mind began asking questions. What happened in real life after the finish of my story? How long did the stallion live? And what about his offspring? Did Hambletonian's fame continue to grow or did it diminish?

Such questions sent me scurrying back to my boxful of notes and mementos gathered years before. "All right!" I said to myself. "Now is the time to make a separate volume of *One Man's Horse*. And now I can add a postlude with lots of pictures to trace Hambletonian's influence as the progenitor of all the great trotters of the world."

To my joy Dorothy Haas, my present-day editor, was completely in accord with the idea. For she too felt the same curiosity as I had to know more about what happened after the story ended.

Sky-Borne

FEET PLANTED WIDE in the peaty earth, William Rysdyk straightened from his ditching, rolled up his sleeves, took a red bandanna from his pocket and swabbed the sweat from under his beard.

A rugged, muscle-powered man he was, and now he flexed and stretched like some Atlas propping the sky with the pillars of his arms. Scraggly brows shadowed deep blue eyes, and a full black beard grew down to hide the first two buttons of his linsey-woolsey shirt. His ears, rather large, came to a point at the top to give him the look of a leprechaun.

But Rysdyk was quite the opposite—a solitary man of the earth, a Dutchman working hard with animals and crops in the fields of his two employers, Jonas Seely and Peter Townsend.

Before going back to his digging, Rysdyk jutted his beard to the sky and took a weather reading. What he saw held him transfixed.

9

Appearing from nowhere at all a cloud, massive and dark, topped Sugar Loaf Mountain, then in one motion scudded up to the sun and inked it out. The cloud was clean-formed, in the likeness of a stallion—a stallion trotting four-square across the mountain. He was veined in light and his mane spurted licks of flame and his tail was fringed in fire and his nostrils blew sparks so that the sky was all horse and the valley all his shadow.

"Ai, yai, yai!" breathed William Rysdyk. "Yonder he is. Himself! Who else?"

So lost was he in the spectacle that the voice of his employer fell on him like a weight.

"Rysdyk!"

Startled, the hired man came back to himself. He looked over his shoulder to see stately Jonas Seely astride his grey gelding.

"Excuse, sir?" William Rysdyk asked, puckering his lips as if he were saying O.

Seely's voice filled the valley, then the mountain took it up and buffeted the sound back. "Rysdyk! June is blowing across the land!"

What kind of talk was this! How could a month go blowing? The Dutchman stood with questioning eyes, watching his boss gesture toward the upland pasture.

"The steers are sleek and stout," he pronounced, "and the gloss on the Alderney bull is high. Friday next, if Mister Townsend can spare you, we will drive them to New York to market."

The hired man nodded absently, as if going to market were no adventure at all.

"And I have also come to make a survey of your progress with the drainage ditch. Lay a footbridge across about here," Seely directed, "about where Sir Luddy's forefeet stand."

"Yah, yah, sir." The answer was a faraway singsong as Rysdyk's gaze was drawn back to the horse-cloud still blotting the sun.

10

"Egad, man!" There was irritation in Mister Seely's voice. It made his face red and his muttonchop whiskers very white. "What holds you in a trance? What is it?"

A work-soiled finger pointed to the sky. Jonas Seely looked, and the phenomenon cast its spell over him, too. He tied the reins in a knot and leaned back, his hands on Sir Luddy's hips. "Hmmm ... strange," he mused, "how man can witch the clouds. I see in them a horse, trotting through fire."

"You too, sir?" The question had a note of admiration in it.

"Aye," Mister Seely spoke almost in a whisper. "The cloud is a ghost-mare from my boyhood."

As the cloud began to fade, William Rysdyk bent to his ditching. Then he thought better of it. Maybe, he said to himself, if I listen nice and polite to Mister Seely's remembrances, he listen maybe to me. "How was she called, sir?" he asked.

"We named her Silvertail because of the tuft of silver hairs at the root of her tail."

"And does it yet grieve you for her?"

"No, no. Not now! That was some forty years ago."

Rysdyk wanted to continue the talk. He wanted to tell about *his* horse. Yet try as he would, he couldn't think of more questions to ask. He returned to his work, fiercely digging and pitching.

But Jonas Seely did not wait for questions. He was bursting with memories. "I'm minded of the time Silvertail traveled seventy-five miles to market and back in a single day." He glanced down at his hired hand for an "Ai yai yai." When none came, he went on. "And my father and I were riding double to boot! Of course, I was a mere sprout of a boy at the time. Ten or thereabouts."

"By golly," said William Rysdyk with no emphasis at all.

"Ah, there was a mare! She came by her spirit honestly. Her sire was the Imported Messenger, brought over from England."

"*Messenger?*" Rysdyk dropped his shovel. His head jerked up, his beard parting in the little wind. "Messenger" was a name he knew! "Sir! A question I got to ask."

"Ask!" encouraged Seely.

"When Messenger stomps down the gangplank, what they say about him—it be true?"

"Indeed so. When his ship landed at Philadelphia, the other horses were too weak to walk down the gangplank—"

"And him, sir?"

"He came charging down, lifting two grooms off their feet, up and down like pump handles. Then he ran through the streets of Philadelphia, the grooms dangling along like birds on a string."

Rysdyk chuckled, wishing he had been there to see.

"Silvertail was like him!" Seely said proudly. Suddenly he was embarrassed by all this talk of himself and his mare. He turned kindly to his hired man. "Did you ever see a horse that fastened itself on your memory?"

Rysdyk stood dumb. He looked about awkwardly, letting the gelding lick the salt from his hand. "Ach, my words they get altogether mixed in a heap." He glanced up at the cloud. And wonder of wonders, the stallion was on fire again, high-tailing across the sky.

"Mister Seely!" Rysdyk shouted, the words now spilling out in a rush. "Oncet some water I was pumping up and a horse and rider come by me. And I pump up only one of my buckets. I forget my mother is needing both. I just stand. The horse—in his eye a look he had. How do you say in English?"

"The look of eagles?"

"Yah! The eagle look he had!" Rysdyk nodded, the chords in his neck swelling. "Now comes it, sir! Now comes the best part." His voice hushed. "The evening dark is pulling down already, but the rider turns his horse and they make for me. And they stop. And I water the horse from our own drinking pail. He sucks it up, with the eagle-look still looking."

Rysdyk was trembling. "And when he gallops away, I just stand. Yah, I just stand until the mama calls, 'Will-yum! Pump out!' And I to her yell, 'There comes no water out!' and she yells, 'Pump! You not pumping!' "

Now it was the hired man's turn to be embarrassed. He looked down at his big hands. "You think I stay just at the talking?" he asked. "I got to hurry myself along with the ditching."

"No, no. Wait! I find myself curious as to the stallion's name. Do you know it?"

A deep guttural laugh accompanied the answer. *"Do I got his name?* It stabs like a dagger inside my head."

"Speak out!"

"Hamble-tonian it was. He got it from Hamble-ton, a race course in England."

"And the rider?"

"He was called by the name Bishop. And the horse, he was the son of Messenger."

Mister Seely leaped out of the saddle, grasping William Rysdyk by the shoulders, shaking him until the hairs in his beard seemed to jump up and down like wire springs. "Bishop's Hambletonian!" he thundered. "Egad, Rysdyk, my father bred my Silvertail to your Hambletonian!" He held out his hand. "Let us salute the blood of Messenger." Solemnly employer and workman shook hands while overhead the cloud wisped off into nothing and the brassy sun came out.

Butcher's Nag

William Rysdyk forgot the cloud image on his first trip to New York City. To him the journey was good beyond all dreaming. The teamwork between Mister Seely and himself was so nice and precise. They were a matched pair! That Mister Seely, he thought, is not afraid of the work. Here, there, everywhere he is. Herding the cattle out of the brush, away from grazing space, around a hill, keeping them always on the go.

"Boss good!" he kept chuckling to himself, proud of his employer. "Like he was born with a horse under him, he rides."

He had no idea that Jonas Seely was equally proud of his hired man. Here was a drover, Mister Seely thought, who prodded the steers with his voice. Not his stick.

Along the way whole families came running when they saw the cloud of dust rising as the cattle clumped toward them. Out of their fields and kitchens they came, waving broad hats and

sunbonnets, shooing the steers, keeping them from turning into the farm lanes and joining their own cattle.

Sometimes they were round-faced Dutch folk who stood in shy embarrassment when pompous Mister Seely rode up. But when they heard the familiar singsong of William Rysdyk's speech, they invited him and Mister Seely too into their snug, whitewashed houses.

"Come," they would urge, "is nooning time. Our Hans and Hendrick the cattle for you can watch. The eating is ready. It gives runderslappen and fresh crullers."

Such good food it was! Even Mister Seely, used to porridge and cold mutton at noon, passed his plate for second helpings of runderslappen, the thick-sliced beef spiced with apples and cloves. Often there was lentil soup, too, made with pigs' feet and sausage, and for dessert a huge bowl of crullers, filled from a bottomless crock.

And so the employer on horseback and the drover afoot made a pleasant junket of the journey southward along the Hudson River until they approached New York.

Once in the hurry-scurry of the city, however, William Rysdyk was a man lost. The city sounds boxed his ears and bewildered his mind. By day he felt himself a frighted hound, hugging his master's heels. By night in his bed in the Bull's Head Tavern, the city vehicles and the river craft seemed to rumble over his very body. He could hardly breathe for the hurting of the noise.

Afterward, he remembered very little of the city itself. He recalled, as in a dream, the livestock parade with bands playing and bells ringing and people's heads sprouting out of windows. And he remembered he was in the parade, holding the lead shank of the Alderney bull. But of the sea of people on either side of him he remembered not one face. Of Pearl Street and Wall Street and Broadway he could recall not one building. Of the awarding of a silver trophy to Mister Seely he remembered only that the sun glanced off it, almost blinding him. The words said he could not remember. They were mere puffs of smoke.

But with the parade over and the cattle sold and now the joyous prospect of going home, everything suddenly came sharp and clear. William Rysdyk was in the box of the cart, alone now that the prize bull had been sold at auction. And Mister Seely, sitting on the driver's seat beside Butcher Kent, was holding the trophy his Alderney had won.

17

"I'll drop you and your man at the Bull's Head," Mister Kent was saying. "You know, of course, that you are expected at the turtle feast of the Agricultural Society this evening. It is my duty to arrange the seating of the dignitaries."

Mister Kent looked for and got no answer, for he was making a great flourish with his whip. And the rough-coated mare that drew the cart was taking off at a good gait, picking her way through the streets in elegant style. Dogs and cats and a big fat goose retreated in alarm.

"For an old mare," Mister Seely said loudly, leaning forward in pleasure, "she is quick and trappy."

Butcher Kent nodded. "Aye!" he shouted, "and she should be! I got her of a banker who paid six hundred dollars for her. Under saddle she twice trotted the Union Course at a two-fifty clip."

"Eh?" grunted Seely in astonishment.

William Rysdyk held onto the sides of the cart, spraddling his feet to steady himself as they lunged and lurched over the rough streets.

"And where did the banker get her?"

"From a fish peddler who'd paid out a paltry sum for her."

Mister Seely's next words jerked out to the motion of the cart. "There's something about her head . . . and her way of going . . . and the angling of her hock . . . ." But the wind scattered his words.

"The banker," Mister Kent offered, "gave me no papers with her. Nor a name. We call her Butcher's Nag from her habit of pulling up lame after a day's work."

As if the mare had overheard, she began limping, and by the time they reached the Bull's Head Tavern she was a pitiable sight with her uneven gait.

William Rysdyk jumped out of the cart, waiting for Mister Seely, but his employer was deep in thought.

18

"What of her lameness?" he asked, looking at Kent.

"I know not the particulars." The man's eyes glinted as he slowly returned the whip to its socket, sensing a deal in the air. "I was told there was an accident," he replied, measuring his words. "The mare had good cause to shy and run away, and the chaise swung into a tree. As I heard it, she got her leg caught in one of the wheels and she herself was thrown to the paving stones."

"The result a spavin?"

"A slight one," nodded Mister Kent, forgetting about the seating of the dignitaries. "Only when she is tired would you observe it."

"I find it somewhat of a smart," Mister Seely said, plucking at the tufts of his muttonchop whiskers, "to see a mare put to work with a bad spavin."

"The spavin is nothing, I tell you. In the morning, rested, she will go sound."

The question Mister Kent looked for came more quickly than he expected.

"What will you take for your Butcher's Nag?" Seely inquired.

From the stables beyond the inn, two grooms came up, listening, awaiting orders.

"Go on about your business," Mister Kent told them not un-kindly. Then turning to Mister Seely, "I'll take a hundred and thirty-five for her."

Looking at the mare, William Rysdyk swallowed. A hundred and thirty-five taler! Why, she was over the fifteen. Over the twenty, maybe.

"It is too steep a price," Mister Seely was saying without any rise in his voice. "You know it full well. And I know it."

"P'raps so. P'raps so. But I too bought her with the same spavin. And, I might add, at the same figure. Now I really must be off."

Mister Seely got down from the cart, thinking. "The turtle feast tempts me," he said, yawning, "but I believe I will rest against the morrow's journey." He lowered his voice. "Should the mare go sound by noontide, I will buy her at your price. She might make a good brood mare."

The two men shook hands to seal the agreement. Then William Rysdyk and Mister Seely stood watching as the mare limped away, until she and her cart were swallowed by the lengthening shadows.

𝔄 𝔅argain 𝔐ade

Precisely at the hour of noon, Mister Kent appeared at the Bull's Head Tavern with the mare tied to the tail of a wagon.

"Here she is! And sound as a dollar," he announced to Mister Seely as he untied her and walked her about. "Note," he said, "how the swelling has subsided and the lameness with it."

Mister Seely tilted his head, watching to see if the mare placed her weight evenly on all four feet. "Hmm," he mused in unbelief, for her feet touched the ground smartly, each stroke quick and strong.

William Rysdyk stared in astonishment as he saw ten- and twenty-dollar gold pieces go from Mister Seely's pocket into the cupped hands of Mister Kent. And, dumbfounded, he heard the calm words, "Here are the gold pieces you paid out for the Alderney; your own dollars come back to roost!"

On the way out of the city, Mister Seely rode Sir Luddy and William Rysdyk led the mare. It was true about her going sound after a night's rest. She raised her knee and hock well, thrusting her legs forward and backward in a smooth stroke.

Not a word passed between the two men until they had crossed King's Bridge over the Spuyten Duyvil Creek and were out on the Harlem Valley Road.

Then Mister Seely made an eyeshield of his hand. He looked ahead and he looked behind. "Whoa, Rysdyk!" he commanded when he had made certain no one was anywhere in sight. "Now look! Does the butcher's nag have a star? Very small? High under the forelock?"

Quick hands lifted the greying lock of hair. "Yah, shure."

"And is one foreleg more roan than bay?"

"Shure, shure. Already I see it in New York."

"Look sharp! Does she have a fine white coronet on her near, no, on her off hind leg?"

William Rysdyk walked around and observed. "Yah, on her off side, sir, if you look hard."

The questions streamed on. "Look, Rysdyk! On the neck under her mane. A quirl?"

"How say you?"

"A quirl—a spot where the hair grows frowardly?"

William Rysdyk lifted the mane. And there, underneath, just as Mister Seely had said, was a little spot where the hair grew wayward. "Shure! Shure! The hairs they turn themselves around!"

Mister Seely threw back his head and slapped his thigh. "It's the same mare all right," he chuckled, as if enjoying some secret joke. "The same mare brother Peter rode. She could be a vixen, Rysdyk, if it were not for that bad spavin."

"Yah?"

"Now leg up on her. You're not so old as your beard makes you out. I wager she'll feel younger as she gets to traveling country roads instead of cobblestones. Here, lead her alongside. That's it.

Now put your foot in my stirrup and leap aboard. No need of a bit and bridle. She'll stay close to Sir Luddy for companionship."

William Rysdyk vaulted onto the mare's back and snugged his knees into place. He felt her alert. And all of a sudden he was elevated in spirit as well as body. "Ach!" he cried in ecstasy. "I feel myself big. Look once, sir. By golly, she stands me good! You think maybe I fit her all right?"

Mister Seely's nod left no doubt.

For the first time in his life William Rysdyk was riding alongside Mister Seely. For the first time he was astride a fine trappy animal instead of a broad-backed work horse. As they journeyed along he could not help comparing the mare with Sir Luddy. "That Luddy, he is jughead alongside her," he said to himself. "By criminy, with her rough coat yet she's beautiful like anything."

They rode on in silence, following the silver river, going slowly along like the steamboat lazing downstream.

At last Mister Seely broke into the quiet. "This mare without a name," he said as they ambled along, "is a great-granddaughter of Messenger."

"So? That explains it why she could go around the Union Course so quick?"

"That is but part of the reason."

"Yah?"

"Yes, but a part."

A flock of wild pigeons flew low over their heads, the noise of their wings shutting out the talk.

"How you going to say, sir?" reminded William Rysdyk when the whistle of bird wings had gone by.

Jonas Seely laughed loud and long until the blood deepened in his face. It made his white stock look whiter than the underside of the pigeons. Could be a stroke striking him! the hired man thought in alarm. Then he sighed with relief as Mister Seely went on.

"The mare you ride," he chortled, "had no time to wait for a name. She was a runaway at every chance." His laughter broke out afresh. "One day my brother limped home from a ride and sold her off quick as scat before his bruises had a chance to heal."

"Yah?" asked William Rysdyk, his eyebrows crawling up and up his forehead.

"The wings on her heels came from—"

"Yah? Yah?"

"They came from her grandsire and granddam." Mister Seely slapped a fly that worried his horse.

William Rysdyk could stand the suspense no longer. Now his face was red, too. "And who *was* they, sir?" he exploded.

"They were," said Jonas Seely, stretching out the words until they snapped into the hired man's face, "they were my Silvertail and your Bishop's Hambletonian."

A gasp came from the black beard. "Bishop's Hamble-tonian!" The hands holding the halter rope began to shake and the bronzed face went ashy grey. With a little cry no more than a dog's whimper, William Rysdyk toppled from the mare's back into the dust of the road.

Like a scalded cat she bolted up the pike, the lead rope snaking out behind her.

Crowbait

The hard fall jolted William Rysdyk to his senses. He scrambled to his feet in time to see the mare going for the river at a full gallop, Mister Seely riding hard to head her off.

"Whoa-oa!" called William Rysdyk, running, stumbling, breaking through the underbrush. "Whoa-oa, girl!"

And then all of a sudden the steamboat that had been gliding so swanlike downstream let go an ear-splitting blast. Pitchy smoke and fire spurted from her funnel. To the mare it must have seemed the end of the world.

Rearing and wheeling in panic, she flew back toward the road, only to be met by a traveling peddler who had joined the pursuit. He was brandishing a rifle, flailing the air like a windmill. Fear rooted the mare. On all sides she was threatened. The monstrous whistling boat on her right, Sir Luddy charging on her left, and now this live windmill coming straight at her.

Only one sound tried to soothe. "Whoa-oa, girl. Whoa-oa, girl," came Rysdyk's singsong as he slowed toward her.

Like a weathercock when the wind turns she skewed in his

direction. But all in a split second her bad leg caught in a tree root and she fell thrashing and struggling in the brush.

As she lay wedged in a little hollow where scrub willow grew rank, the three men stood over her, shaking their heads. It took all three to tear and cut the brush away and roll her onto her belly.

With a low moan she got to her feet and stood there, helpless, her body drenched in sweat.

"Now my advice," twanged the peddler in mock sympathy, "is to put the old girl out o' her misery. She's old and spavined. Nothing but crowbait. Tell ye what I'll do," he said, fondling the barrel of his rifle. "I'll help ye with the unpleasant business. Then I'll show ye my wares. Got some mighty fine clocks and firearms."

A little shivering went over the mare. Her lower lip hung loose and trembling. She tried to put her weight on the hurt leg, then flinched in pain.

"I fear the peddler is right," agreed Mister Seely, still puffing from exertion. "It is the merciful thing to do."

The mare's eyes looked at William Rysdyk, and he caught his own reflection in their soft reproach. "Please, sir," he said, turning to Mister Seely. "Why do we got to do this?" He cast about him for some excuse and found it in the setting sun. "Look, sir. It comes already evening. Her hock only is outgiven. She could hobble with us along to a farmhouse maybe. There I make her a bed up. Tomorrow we see how goes it with her."

It was a long speech for William Rysdyk. He wiped the sweat from his forehead, waiting to hear what Mister Seely would say.

"Well, now," replied Mister Seely, loosening his cravat, "it will do no harm to wait. Hasty actions are oft regretted. Come. Let us proceed."

The peddler whistled between his wide-set teeth. "Crowbait," he spat, as if the word took in men and mare both. Disgustedly, he stomped back to his cart, threw in his rifle, and drove off.

The first farmhouse that came into view could have been a hovel for all it mattered to the weary travelers. But it was, instead, a homey place nosing up out of lilac bushes and honeysuckle. The farmer, a tall, loose-jointed man, had to stoop a little to come out of his doorway. He walked toward them jerkily, as if his legs and arms worked from puppet strings.

After welcoming the strangers, he examined the swelling on the mare's hock. " 'Pears to me like she's old and done for," he said. "But she's more'n welcome to a bundle of hay and a bed in my cow barn."

"We shall be grateful to you," Mister Seely answered.

"Tsk," the farmer said, suddenly remembering, "Hetty, my woman, would like fer you folks to stay, too. Our house," he laughed, "looks little but she bulges fer comp'ny."

Then he thought a moment. "You ain't asked it, I know, but we got us a pined cemetery for our own animals down the road a piece." He thumbed toward the mare. "If she ain't better by morning, ye're welcome to my musket. And you can leave her there a-sleepin' if you got a mind to."

"Why is it always got to be a shooting?" William Rysdyk kept asking himself as he made a warm bran poultice and tied up the mare's leg. "Why is it?"

Neither he nor Mister Seely did justice to the plain supper of wheaten bread, fresh butter, and stewed pumpkin which the farmer's wife set out for them. And they were both up at dawn, hoping some miracle had happened in the night.

There had been no miracle. The mare lay on her side, quite still. When the men talked to her, she struggled to rise, moaning low in her throat. It was with great difficulty that William Rysdyk and the farmer boosted her to her feet.

"Rysdyk," Mister Seely said, his face strained with emotion, "I'm loath to ask what needs doing. But it is better this way. Better for her to sleep in a piney woods than to end her days pulling a butcher's wagon. You did not know her when she was a spirited filly, as I did. Will you do it for me? I'll saddle Sir Luddy while you are gone and meet you down the road."

"Ach, wait! Wait!" William Rysdyk began, but this time he could think of no reason for waiting. His strength suddenly washed out of him. Never in his life had he killed an animal. He who could jack up a wagon with his hands while weaker men rolled the wheel in place, stood limp as a string of herbs.

"I'll fetch my musket," the farmer said with a nervous jerking of his arms. He was in and out of the house, and still William Rysdyk stood.

But at last the waiting seemed worse than the doing. He made himself fasten the lead strap to the mare's halter, made himself shoulder the long-barreled musket. With set face he led her down

the path between the lilacs. He watched her head bent almost to her knees, watched her hobbled, painful step. Without knowing he was doing it, he too limped to her rhythm.

When she struck the road, however, an astonishing change came over her. She began to limber up and her head lifted in interest, sifting the scents and sounds. As they went on toward

27

the conical trees she was walking more firmly than the man who led her, almost pulling him along.

At the entrance to the little clearing in the pines, William Rysdyk halted. "By golly!" he cried out, determination in his eyes, "I will *not* shoot her dead. Here's a mare who will stay in the life!"

He faced about and the mare followed him back to the road, nickering when she caught sight of Sir Luddy ambling toward them. As the two horses met and snuffed nostrils, William Rysdyk looked up between Sir Luddy's ears, directly into Mister Seely's face. "Butcher's Nag goes sound, sir. She comes with us along, please could be?"

Mister Seely blew his nose loud as a trumpet, then made a soft gurgle in his throat as if he wanted to talk but couldn't.

"She will have it pleasant with us? Yah, sir?"

The misty-eyed man could only nod.

"And when deep winter comes and we have it cold and the ground lies shut and hard—she gets shelter? Yah, sir?"

"Yah it is!" Mister Seely smiled through his tears.

Rat-Tail Abdallah

The trip home to Sugar Loaf was slower than the trip to New York. William Rysdyk walked all the way, except downhill. Then Mister Seely dismounted and led the mare while his hired man rode Sir Luddy.

The two men had little to say to each other. There was a bond between them now that made words unnecessary. They let the mare plod along at her own pace, let her stop to rest, nodding on three legs whenever she had a mind to. Meanwhile, William Rysdyk took off his boots and yarn stockings and cooled his aching feet in the grass. After a little while man and mare would be ready to start off again.

At the journey's end it was the men and Sir Luddy who seemed travel weary. The mare appeared a little gaunt and she favored one leg, but her spirit was game.

As they turned into the Seely lane, Sir Luddy gave a loud and joyful neigh. "Here," he snorted quite plainly, "is Home! Green grass growing where grass should grow and shade where shade should be and snug horse barns with doors thrown wide to the sun."

In the weeks that followed, William Rysdyk was a boy with his first pet. He was boy and nurse and doctor too. He pulled off the mare's shoes. He trimmed her bruised and broken hoofs and rubbed them with goose grease. At night he led her down to the drainage ditch, and making a cup of his hands bathed the swollen hock with cool water. Then he turned her loose to walk barefoot in the dewy grass.

There were so many little ways in which William Rysdyk cared for the mare. He crushed her oats and ground her corn, knowing her old nippers and tushes were too worn to grind the hard kernels. And when he found she liked milk, he brought her each evening a little piggin of it, still fragrant and warm.

"Egad!" Mister Seely remarked one day as he saw her capering about in the pasture lot. "She grows most pleasant to look upon— her coat glossed, her eye clear and bold."

"Yah! She feeds hearty, sir," nodded William Rysdyk proudly. "Soon it comes time to step her on the road."

Mister Seely ruminated a moment, roughing up his mutton-chop whiskers. "Hook her up now, Rysdyk. We'll see how she goes."

Once out on the road the Kent mare threw a challenge to every horse they met. She seemed unable to abide hoofbeats behind or hoofbeats ahead. She took the bit and raced down the pike as if she were trotting the Union Course. But with the brush over, she hobbled home, moaning in pain. It was plain to see she would never go the distances again.

And so fingers pointed and heads wagged and voices laughed to scorn. "Ho-ho! A prize Alderney bull for a broken-down butcher's nag!" The words had a sting to them.

Winter came and the ground lay "shut and hard" as William Rysdyk had said it would. And the mare was given shelter.

Her purple-brown eyes, sometimes vixenish, sometimes sad, laid a kind of spell on Mister Seely and his hired man. But they were alone in their feelings. The townfolk could not see in her the look of eagles. It was not given everyone to see. Even Mistress Seely regarded the Kent mare as a bad bargain, taking money from her own till, money that might better have been spent on new carpeting or tea plates, or even a fur muff.

Winter shuffled off and spring came mincing in. And one early June afternoon when William Rysdyk arrived at Sugar Loaf to do the chores, he found Mister Seely sitting on a pile of logs beside the smoke house. "Sit down, Rysdyk," he said, waving his arm toward the logs as if offering a fine plush chair.

William Rysdyk sat. No words were spoken. Nothing happened. Impatiently, he crossed and uncrossed his legs. He had the Jerseys and the Holsteins to bring home. The milking to do. The horse stalls to clean. Then the same chores to be done for his other employer, Mister Townsend.

"I've news," Mister Seely said at last, taking off his hat and letting the wind pick up his milkweed hair.

"News? So?"

"Aye, my brother Ebenezer was here this day."

What news was that! Ebenezer, a brother, comes. "Comes he not often, sir?" William Rysdyk asked.

"Aye. But this day he had the stallion, Old Abdallah, with him."

"Old Abdallah?"

"Old Abdallah. And this day of June, eighteen hundred and forty-eight, the Kent mare was bred to him."

"To Old Abdallah!" William Rysdyk tried to swallow his resentment. It was done, and now no need to make questions, but in his mind he was seeing the coarse and ugly stallion, and the words spat themselves out. "Why, he is old as the Sugar Loaf Mountain, sir."

Mister Seely laughed hollowly. "Not that old, Rysdyk."

"Is he not over the twenty-five, sir?"

"Aye."

William Rysdyk stood up. He began stripping the bark from the logs, venting his anger on them. "The mare is a horse whereon you can be proud, sir. But Old Abdallah..." he could think of no words strong enough. "Old Hollow-Back! Old Rat-Tail!"

"Aye," the answering voice was quiet.

"A big homely head he has."

Mister Seely nodded.

"And hardly no more hairs in his tail as a naked stick."

"I, too, have noted the scraggly tail."

"And his temper it is fierce, sir."

A cat came sidling along, thinning herself against Mister Seely's legs. William Rysdyk saw Abdallah in the cat. His voice rose. "That Abdallah has cat hams, sir."

"So he has. I'd never thought of it just like that. But you forget two things. He can trot. And his dam was a Thoroughbred."

The words floated over and around the hired man, unnoticed.

"And ears so big he has, with sharp points." Suddenly William Rysdyk clapped his hands to his own ears. He smiled a little. "I must to the chores now," he said. "I feel myself not good."

Mister Seely's eyes were on the distance. "When the colt is born, Rysdyk, you'll forget all about Old Ab."

The hired man forced a nod. Heavy-legged, he trudged off toward the upland pasture. "Till seeing," he said. "When the colt comes..." The words tailed off into nothing. It was the will of God, and he hoped it would be the will of God that the foal would not look like Old Abdallah.

The Foaling Spot

William Rysdyk worked in a wrath of energy, hoping the harder he worked the faster time would go; hoping, too, it would help him forget that no-account Abdallah.

Almost a year to wait for the foal!

Slowly the days piled one on top of the other. Days of stooping and lifting and dragging stones to clear a new field for Mister Townsend. Days of plowing and cross-harrowing and pulverizing the land. Days of scattering seed until the very sockets of his arms ached. Rainy days and dusty ones. And blistering days when his beard dripped sweat. Days of making hay when he stopped only to let the work horses blow or to put the nosebag on them. He, too, was a work horse. At night when he pulled off his boots and stockings it sometimes surprised him to see feet and ankles instead of hoofs and hairy fetlocks.

The days grew shorter, cooler. Days of shocking corn. Pulling onions. Heaping turnips. Digging potatoes. Sacking them. Hauling them. Shipping them to market.

Then still and brittle days when icy branches snapped and spooked the horses. In the still days William Rysdyk chopped wood, repaired the plow irons, sharpened the harrow tines, mended harness.

So the seasons went their rounds without stint, without haste. And it was spring again. Spring with white dogwood pricking down the mountainsides and green needles of wheat breaking the soil and mallards swimming in the high creeks. Just like that it came. Spring, and the Kent mare big with foal.

One early morning of May, his dinner in a poke, William Rysdyk clicked the latch of his own gate and set out for the Seely farm. Thinking of the mare, he hastened his steps. Today he would make her stall ready. The good clean bed. The fresh straw. Today it might be. He was glad when a team and wagon pulled alongside and a family on their way to a camp meeting drove him to the Seely gate.

Even before he jumped from the wagon he felt hurried by a strange uneasiness—as if things were somehow different. Yet everything looked just as it did on any other Monday morning. Smoke feathering from the chimney. Newly hung wash skewing and bellying on the line. Chickens picking and pecking in the dooryard. Wagons standing, waiting. Everything the same. Yet somehow different.

He broke into a run, past the woodshed, the stackyard, the corncrib, past the spring house with the milk cans drying in the sun, past the chicken house, the root cellar, to the horse barn.

He looked inside. Sir Luddy was nosing above his stall door, pawing and whinnying for his breakfast. The big-faced work horses, too, were snuffling and snorting to the morning.

Of all the stalls only the mare's was open. Only she was free to come and go. Now her stall was empty. The straw untrampled. Not even a hollowed-out nest to show she had slept in it.

"Just like some other mornings," William Rysdyk told himself. "Yah, I know that. Often it is she sleeps in the grass."

Yet the uneasiness hung onto him. He studied the pasture.

"Where to has she gone?" he asked. "Not far with her bad leg," he answered himself. "Never does she go far."

He picked up some sacking and ran out into the pasture. Except for a broad shadow flung across the field by three oak trees, the sun lay smooth and yellow on the grass. He tried to see into the shadow, but there was only blackness. He thought he heard the mare. He went running toward the knoll where the trees grew, calling to her as he ran. "It comes *me!*" he cried, stumbling over the hummocky ground, leaping across the ditch. Then he slowed. He saw her now, in a spot of sun that pierced the trees.

A sigh of relief escaped him. "She likes to neighbor with the tree trunks," he reminded himself, "to scratch and itch herself on the bark. But why is it the sawhorse there in the pasture? Ach, the Seely boys is up to no good, always leaving around tools and such."

Then suddenly the four stiff legs of the sawhorse scissored.
No. It couldn't be a colt. It could be a deer? No, no.

And yet—? Could it be the little one? It's got to! Nothing else
could so long-legged be. Not a dog. Not a sheep. It's got to!

"Maybe," he said, his voice trembling, "maybe if I sneak up by
them very quiet." He began picking his way carefully on tiptoe,
then changed his mind. "No," he smiled into his beard, "I'll look
like I wasn't even looking." He took a roundabout route, talking
in an undertone as he walked. "A quiet place is this for a foaling.
No eyes prying. No noise. Only wind whispers."

And now he was under the crown of shade with them. Close
enough to study the new-born creature. With curious eyes the colt
turned his head, his mother's milk beaded along the feelers of his
muzzle like tiny seed pearls.

"Ai yai yai!" Rysdyk murmured. It was Old Abdallah's foal all
right, but seeing the colt, he saw in him Messenger charging down
the gangplank, Silvertail trotting the highroad with a man and
a boy on her back, Hambletonian with the look of eagles.

A high baby whinny interrupted his dreams. He smiled at his
foolishness, fondling the creature with his eyes.

"How long you here already, little fellow?"

The nostrils fluttered in answer.

"And how pleases you our world?"

The head tossed.

"So, you high-nose our world, hmm? Or is it you have hunger?"

The mare took up with the colt, licking him, snuffing noses
with him, approving him with high nickers of joy.

"Hush up, mare-mom," William Rysdyk whispered. "Is better
you quit out with that noise. Would you to have the Seely boys
come out with their hollerings and jumpings and their sling-
shots, maybe?"

The Kent mare liked the talk. She did not plant herself between William Rysdyk and her colt. She knew he could be trusted even when his man-hands laid hold of her young one.

"He looks bigger as any newborn, yah, mom? And he keeps his head up, no? And he looks pretty fiery."

Gently he began rubbing the colt with the sacking. "By golly," he laughed as the colt struggled to free himself. "You don't like it being rubbed? Come," he coaxed. "Trusting is what a colt is got to learn. Don't wiggle. What helps you that? Only a drying you get from me."

After the rubbing, William Rysdyk clapped his hands. And to his astonishment the colt bent his knobby little knees and broke into a trot toward his mother.

"It don't hardly seem possible!" William Rysdyk sighed. "Yesterday is a big mare only. Today is a baby trotter by her. Is more eating ready, mare-mom?"

He laughed as the colt began suckling, laughed to see the tiny tail flip-flap. "It tastes? Hmm?" he asked.

A cow bawling to be milked broke into his happiness. He sighed again, more deeply this time. "Who wants going to work when a colt is new borned?"

He gathered up the sacks, turning to go. "I'll make you ready a warm mash," he promised the mare, "but first I must to the house to say the news."

When William Rysdyk looked into his employer's office, Mister Seely was scowling over his ledger.

"Anything amiss?" he asked, peering over his glasses.

"Excuse, sir," William Rysdyk began, twirling his hat nervously, "never was anything like him."

"Like whom? Like what, Rysdyk?"

"Like the colt, sir."

Mister Seely laid his quill aside. "Oh," he said with a smile, "so the Kent mare has foaled. Is everything all right?"

"Yah, shure, shure. Is all right. Herself she did it alone."

"Where are they?"

"Just before the big boulder under the oak trees already."

"A fine foaling spot. Always better foaled in the open."

"Yah, with them everything is fine. The mare chawing the grass and the colt sucking good!"

"Rysdyk!"

"Yah, sir?"

"Our Seely custom is this. Whoever spies a colt first has the naming of him."

"How say you?" The words and their meaning seemed too big for understanding.

A silence came into the room. Somewhere in the house a clock bonged the hour of six. Mister Seely got up and circled the day on the wall calendar. May 5, 1849. Then he stood waiting.

William Rysdyk took a great gulp of air. "I don't even got to think, sir! Already he's got him a name . . . Hamble-tonian!"

Mister Seely tapped his lips, thinking.

"Is too long a handle for a little feller?" the question came haltingly.

"No, no, Rysdyk. Come to think of it, Hambletonian is just right. A name of dignity."

Son of Old Abdallah

William Rysdyk heard the clatter of hoofs above the noise of his sledgehammer. He looked down from the upland pasture where he was repairing fence.

A carriage drawn by two high-stepping blacks came whipping around the bend at full speed with a spotted coach dog running

in attendance. As the horses turned into the Seely lane, William Rysdyk raced downhill, arriving just in time to catch the reins.

Suddenly the dooryard came alive. Geese clacking at the coach dog. The coach dog barking at the Seely cats. The blacks neighing and bugling to the Kent mare, whose outline they saw in the distance.

Rysdyk studied the four men as they climbed down from the carriage. Two he recognized. Big John Doughty, the banker, and Israel Toothill, owner of the ironworks. Two he had never seen. One was a little snipe of a man with a slender bill-nose pointing downward. The other was pranked out in a tight-waisted carriage coat with elegant buttons, big as twenty-dollar gold pieces. The coat was too warm for the day. The man within steamed like the horses, his waved forelock clinging damply to his face.

"Gentlemen," Mister Seely shouted above the din, "I am deeply honored. You find me in my house slippers, about to join Mistress Seely in the evening meal. You will sup with us, of course?"

39

The man with the long bill of a nose squinted up at the sun. "Afraid not, Seely," he said, his voice full of high harsh notes. "We've one more stop to make before sundown."

William Rysdyk took a long time tying the lines to the hitching post. Ain't only one man, he thought, it's four. It wonders me. Maybe only they are going to build up a new schoolhouse. But maybe...it could be the colt!

He felt a jerking at his farm frock. Turning, he saw Mister Seely's nephew, his mouth full of green apple but talking anyway, spouting a volley of questions.

"Sh!" William Rysdyk raised his forefinger, pressing it against his pursed lips. He ran into the tool shed and came out with the grindstone and scythe, setting the stone as near the huddle of men as he dared.

"Yourself you turn it," he whispered to the boy. "Watch how the sparks spritz when I make sharp the blade."

The boy turned the crank, fascinated by the flinty sparks. The noise was only a little noise. Rysdyk could listen now.

"We are a committee of four," the banker was saying as he centered the diamond pin in his neckcloth, "and it is our pleasurable duty to line up entries for the matinee trotting races in New York City this fall."

Mister Seely's thumbs were in his trouser pockets, his eyes on Sugar Loaf Mountain, blue-humped in the distance. "Gentlemen, I'm afraid we have no entries this year. Sir Luddy is just a middling goer." He looked from one face to another. "Not since the days of Silvertail have we had a horse that could go the pace and stay the distance. But while you gentlemen are here, I'd be honored with your opinion on a colt by Old Abdallah out of the granddaughter of Silvertail. He's rising four months now."

"Hmmm..." the driver in the splendid coat unbuttoned his

40

enormous gold buttons. He took his watch from his waistcoat and opened it. He showed it to Mister Doughty, the banker.

Four watches came out, the minutes compared.

The decision seemed to rest with Mister Toothill, the iron-monger, as all eyes fastened on him. William Rysdyk studied the man. He was built much like a kangaroo, stout of trunk and leg, with a head that pinched up into nothing as if all the strength had gone into the body. "We could spare ten minutes," he said.

"Come along Rysdyk!" Mister Seely called, "and bring a measure of oats with you. Son, you may come, too."

The men waited, talking about the rain needed, about the Erie Railroad to New York. "Why, she averages nigh twenty miles an hour!" one was saying when William Rysdyk came up to them.

"Rysdyk is my right hand," Mister Seely explained. "He's the only one who can catch the colt."

The men looked at the patched homespun trousers, at the pointed ears, as they followed along, trying without success to keep up with the long strides of Seely's hired man.

Under the oak trees the mare and the colt stood head to tail, switching flies for each other. But when they saw a drove of strangers coming at them, they took off at a bold trot.

William Rysdyk walked away from the fleeing pair, looking skyward as if seeking birds instead of horses to grain. Gradually the colt and the mare changed their course, coming now at a walk toward him. "I will lay out the way it is," he told them. "Now comes a bunch of men. They just stand and look and only make talk. Then they give each other the hand. I don't care for it too, but soon is over. Yah?"

The words were so low-pitched the mare and the colt had to come near and nearer to catch the ups and downs in his voice. Step by step they came until he could lay hold on the colt's halter.

He offered each a palmful of oats for obedience. Then he led the colt to the men, the mare following.

"Uncle!" the Seely boy screamed. "I'm going to be sick!"

Mister Seely excused himself and walked very swiftly toward the outhouse, towing the child. "Too many green apples," he muttered under his breath.

With Mister Seely gone, the men turned their attention on the colt. They spoke freely, as if the hired man were deaf and dumb. But their remarks hit him across the face, lightly at first, then in sharp whiplashes.

"Too high on the legs," said the banker, pulling his plaid waistcoat over his paunch. "No elegance of form."

"Rough made, I should say," piped Henry Spingler, the little snipe of a man. "Note how ungraceful the neck, how large and coarse the head."

"And the ears!" agreed the greatcoated gentleman, stifling a laugh, "long and pointed, like those of a donkey."

"His hips appear higher to me than his shoulders," Mister Toothill put in. "And his tail a mere switch."

Their words lashed on, cutting deeper and deeper.

"Might make a chunk horse for hauling heavy loads," Mr. Doughty offered.

Fat puffy hands and big-knuckled skinny ones felt all the way down the colt's legs, felt of his hindquarters.

"Cat hams!" pronounced the banker.

William Rysdyk caught his breath. His very own words snapping back at him!

Now the men were laughing and joking, clapping each other on the back. "He couldn't beat a calf in a mile and a half," said one. " 'If the leaven's no good,' " Henry Spingler recited, " 'the loaf won't rise, and if the sire's coarse, the colt's likewise.' "

The man with the handsome coat elbowed the ironmonger. "Apt to be a stumblebum," he roared in laughter. "Apt to trip over every molehill."

William Rysdyk let his gaze travel over the colt. To him he was all power and pride. Hips higher than shoulders? Yah, shure. To give speed. Switch tail? Yah, shure. Still a suckling he is. Give the little feller time. In every bone and fiber he saw strength and power. No weakness anywhere. He looked at the tiny star on the forehead, no bigger than a snowflake. He glanced now at the overdressed men, their diamond scarf pins, their gold buttons.

"Ach!" He clenched his fist. "In their looking glasses they should be looking! Needle legs and scrapbag bodies and darning-egg heads!"

The colt, too, seemed annoyed by the talk. He leaned toward the men, his mouth opening now in a great cavernous yawn. In that simple gesture he dismissed them and their fribbling.

When Mister Seely rejoined the group, the men sheared their words like women trimming off the extra crust from a pie.

"He's the son of Old Abdallah, all right," the banker said.

"Yes, sir!" the others agreed. "The son of Old Abdallah. No mistaking."

On the way back to the house the greatcoated man had a trifling accident. He caught his instep-strap on a tree root, and when it snagged free that august gentleman went flat on his buttons in the drainage ditch. He made quite a splash.

It was fortunate for William Rysdyk that a blasting toot from the evening train coincided with the loud explosion of his laughter. "Who now is the stumblebum?" he muttered to himself.

Later, in the stackyard with the men gone, he was still chuckling over the incident. But as he stood atop the strawstack pitching down the straw, an idea fastened itself on his mind. He thrust the pitchfork into the stack, the tines going in deep.

"Maybe," his eyes narrowed in thought, "there is maybe a scheme in the men. It's maybe they think I tell Mister Seely so they buy the colt cheap."

The more he thought about it, the more the idea festered. The committee must have liked Hambletonian. "High on the legs means leggy," he kept saying as he finished his chores. "Leggy colt means speed. Yah! It now comes sharp to me. They make a donkey of Hambletonian for to buy him cheap."

After this visit whenever a stranger came to the Seely place, William Rysdyk was in a panic. He hid the colt and the mare in the spattered shade of the oak trees, tying them there so they couldn't trot out and show bright bay against the green. Then he managed to work within earshot of the visitor. But his work was wasted. If he culled potatoes, he put the little ones with the big. If he split wood for the kitchen, it turned out to be kindling instead of stove wood. If he cleaned stalls, he threw out the clean straw instead of the soiled.

Men did come to look at the colt. Some poked fun at the big ears and the Abdallah head. Others just looked and said little. It was these who worried William Rysdyk most. One night when he had finished his chores, he could stand it no longer.

"I can't hold it out!" he told the colt. "Some way I got to buy you."

Colt=at=Heel

Before his courage petered away, William Rysdyk marched swiftly up to the dooryard of the Seely residence. His mind was made up! He washed his face and hands at the pump, dousing the cold water over his head, taking a great mouthful of it, then fountaining it over a dusty bed of catmint. With awkward fingers he smoothed his hair and combed his beard. He cleaned his boots on the scraper. Then, shivering in excitement, he presented himself at the door.

"The gentleman is in?" he asked the hired girl.

Mehitabel Tiffet had a voice with a growl in it. "He ain't done with his coffee," she said, eyeing him sharply.

"I wait here by the well. I got to speak private with him."

As he waited, playing his finger along the coiled rope, he tried to plan what he would say. Why is it? he thought. With the animals in the fields, I feel myself big. To lift, no stones is too heavy. To dig, no ditches is too deep. But, ach, inside houses I shrink myself. Even my muscles weazen down little. To pea-size they get.

He squirmed, toeing his foot against the well, feeling small and green and young.

The door opened and a hand flung out, holding a plate. "Leftovers," Mehitabel barked, "but they help stay the hunger."

William Rysdyk took the food. A gray slice of mutton had gone cold and tallowed to the plate. Beside it humped a cold potato. He tried to eat, but the tallow reminded him of the goose grease he used on the horses' hoofs.

Looking around and seeing no one in the gathering dusk, he put the plate at his feet. Then low in his throat, so Mehitabel would not hear, he called, "Come, kitling, kitling, kitling."

A barn cat streaked out from the shadows, followed by a parade of four black kittens with stove-poker tails. They maneuvered for position around the plate, then sharp white teeth went to work and four little penwiper tongues and one big one swabbed the plate clean.

As Mehitabel's footsteps came thudding to the door, William Rysdyk snatched up the plate, scattering the cats back into the shadows.

"Kinder hungry, wasn't ye?" Mehitabel's voice softened as she took the plate. "The mister—he is done with his coffee now. Has to have his three cups every night. Come in."

Rysdyk walked quickly through the kitchen and pantry, his nostrils wrinkling at the smells of vinegar and mutton. He followed the direction-flag of Mehitabel's finger through a dark hallway to a brightly glowing room. He took one step across the threshold, then stood frozen in the doorway, like a rabbit cornered by a beam of light.

A lamp burning with an uneven flame made a white pool on the desk, then flung great shadows on the wall. One of the shadows was Mister Seely winding the wag-on-the-wall clock, pulling down the weight cord.

As William Rysdyk waited, hesitating, a small figure brushed past him and burst into the room. "Uncle! Look at the pictures I made."

Mister Seely turned around, surprise in his look. "Oh," he said, spying William Rysdyk over the head of his nephew, "come to the light and let us both study the pictures."

"What for pictures have you?" the hired man asked the boy, with no question in his voice at all. How could he hold his mind on pictures? His eyes looked through them, seeing the colt instead, the big promise in him. A stallion grown. Muscles bulging. Veins big and branching like rivers on a map.

Mister Seely duteously praised the pictures and dismissed the boy. "Now then." His eyes went to William Rysdyk's as he settled himself comfortably in a chair by the desk. He picked up his pen, fluting the feather with his thumb, and waited.

"In your office-room, sir, it don't make right to bother you."

"No bother, Rysdyk. Speak up."

But suddenly the man could not speak, nor even breathe. There was a tightness in his chest and the room seemed to be closing in on him. If he were only out of doors! "Can you, sir—can you once to the pasture lot come?"

"Is anything wrong?"

"No, no. Everything fine."

"Then whatever it is, Rysdyk, say it here."

Say it here, say it here, the clock repeated. And all at once the tight feeling in his chest gave way and the words came tumbling out like water over a mill wheel.

"The colt sir!" he cried. "The colt! Before comes another man to look, I should buy him!"

"You? You? Buy him?"

"Yah, sir. *Who else care like me?*" the tense voice pleaded. "The committee, they make little of him. His ears. Donkey ears. I got donkey ears, too."

He came close to Mister Seely, placing one hand on the desk. "I was godoopt, ach, I mean baptized, here in America. I was godoopt for William of Orange, the same one where Orange County got its name. But I am a Dutchman. Of me everybody makes little. Of the colt, too." He took a deep breath, then blurted, "Is it fine with you if I buy?"

Mister Seely's gaze went to the ceiling. He found a box-elder bug in the splash of light and sat staring at the bug as if it got in the way of his thinking.

"I make a question, sir," reminded his hired man. "Couldn't I got an answer?"

The box-elder bug fell to the desk, Jonas Seely's glance falling with it. "Where would you stable him?" he asked.

"My chicken shed, sir, what Mister Townsend give me, I going to fix up into a barn."

"And what are your plans for the colt?"

"I drive him. And the wind, she whistles by our donkey ears. And we whistle by . . ." William Rysdyk's blue eyes danced with a sudden idea. "And we whistle by Mister Toothill and Mister Doughty and the man what looks like a snipe bird." He laughed deep in his throat.

"What if the colt prove slow and sluggish?"

"It couldn't be."

"You expect both speed and stamina?"

"How could it else? He is deep-made in his heart place."

"Pull up a chair and sit down. Let us ponder a moment."

The chair scraped across the carpet. William Rysdyk perched himself on the edge of it. "My mind is up-made," he said hoarsely. "The littler feller gets into me here, sir." He patted his linsey-woolsey shirt. "If he goes from the pasture lot . . ." His eyes studied a crimson rose in the carpet.

"What then?"

"Then"—the hired man's voice trembled and his beard quivered —"I would like the meadowlark be. The meadowlark who comes back to her field and finds her nest and younkers plowed under by

48

rough hands. Only," he sighed after a little silence, "the meadowlark could sing herself out of the pain. With me it only could stay
inside."

"Come, come, Rysdyk. I must admit I've been thinking of selling,
but you are carrying your dreams too far."

There! He knew it! The boss was going to sell. William Rysdyk hurried his words. "I got a little money, sir, but you give no answer. Could I buy or couldn't I buy?"

Mister Seely let his mind go back to the gold pieces he had paid out for the crippled mare. He turned down the wick of the lamp as if his thoughts might show in his face. She might have a better colt in the future, he was thinking. Maybe one. Maybe two. The postmaster had already offered seventy-five dollars for her. As for the son of Old Abdallah, he might bring a hundred dollars, odd-looking as he was.

He watched the box-elder bug swing up on his paper cutter. His thoughts went on to the drought, to the crops drying. There would be none of the little extras from New York this year. Only the necessaries.

Aloud he said, "The winter will be lean."

"By my place I am already tucked in good, sir. Roots and apples in the cellar already. What matters it to eat turnips of last year's growth?"

Mister Seely did not answer for a long time. "I would have to sell the mare, too," he said at last. "Ever since she came limping through the gate, Mistress Seely has been twitting me to sell her. Yes, they would both have to go. The mare with colt-at-heel."

William Rysdyk leaped to his feet. "By golly! Is better still! Mare-mom too!" He mouthed the sound of the words, "Colt-at-heel, colt-at-heel." He began reaching into his pockets, but all he had in them, he knew, were three big copper pennies and a handkerchief, quite dirty.

"I have along but three coppers with me," he said, "but by my chicken shed in an old teapot I got twenty-five taler."

A smile of pity played about Mister Seely's lips. "I could let you have one of the work horses for that," he said, "but for the

50

mare and colt it would be one hundred and fifty dollars."

The house noises suddenly grew loud and distinct. A rocker creaking on a loose floorboard. Mice skittering in the walls. Against these little noises the hard metal dollars jangled in William Rysdyk's head.

"A hundred and fifty taler!"

"For twenty-five dollars you could have the work horse, Rysdyk. He has perhaps fifteen good years left in him. Perhaps twenty."

The words were lost. A hundred and fifty taler! The hired man sighed deeply, then rose from his chair.

"Rysdyk!" Irritation showed in Mister Seely's voice, but it was as if he were irritated with himself, too. "Rysdyk," he repeated, "you would be better off with the work horse. And I would be better off selling the pair to a pleasantly situated farmer. He could get one or two foals from the mare, and the colt would make him a good wagon horse."

Over and over William Rysdyk turned the coppers in his hand. "They look so few," he said, discouragement heavy in his voice. "Couldn't you a little cheaper make it?"

The annoyance in Mister Seely's voice grew. "One hundred and twenty-five is my limit. If I sell at that figure, I am beetle-headed. If you buy at that figure, you are. The work horse, now . . ."

"Better I go home, sir, and put the head on the pillow. After a sleep I know for sure."

In the morning William Rysdyk did know. It was sunup and the two men stood facing each other in the barnyard. Morning lay wet on the fence rails and on the leaves of the trees.

"My mind, it is up-made, sir!" William Rysdyk said with a resolute look in his eye. "Only one question I could want to ask."

Mister Seely waited.

"The money it grows slow. With the wages of ten taler a month from you and six taler from Mister Townsend, how long time I got to pay?"

"As long as you like, Rysdyk," Mister Seely said kindly. It hurt him to take the money at all. But he had set his price. "I'm glad the two will be with you," he added.

As calloused hands counted out twenty-five silver dollars, a faraway look came into Mister Seely's eyes. "Where the ramp meets the barn door," he said, "a secret vault lies beneath. There, wrapped in a worn hearth rug and covered with a piece of oiled cloth, is Silvertail's saddle. It now belongs to you."

Slowly Jonas Seely turned and walked into the house and up the stairs. He stood by the upper hall window and watched his hired man disappear into the vault. He watched him come out with Silvertail's saddle and lay it on the mare's back. Watched him ride out of the lane with a colt skittering along at heel.

For a time he stood there until the three creatures smalled and were lost to view.

Rysdyk's Big Bull

The Kent mare with colt-at-heel faced the morning and the bigness of it. It belonged to them. The whole of it. Earth and sky and mountain, and leaves swirling and goldfinches swinging on weed stems until a body dizzied just watching. Sometimes a madcap wind tossed a shower of hickory nuts on their heads. This sent the colt scampering off until his mother whickered him back.

There was so much for the colt to do! Milkweed fluff to blow to smithers, blinking frogs to out-stare, then to flip with his muzzle until he jumped them out of sight.

"Ai yai yai," sighed William Rysdyk as he slid down from the mare's back to lead her a while. "Hambletonian and mare-mom. *It ain't only one kind of joy, it's two!*"

They passed houses with featherbeds airing and houses sending out spicy odors of fall preserving, passed cornfields with men shocking corn and gangs of blackbirds squawking over dropped kernels. But William Rysdyk neither saw nor heard nor smelled autumn. For his eyes there was only the colt trotting beside his mother, for his ears only the patter of hoofs on the road, for his nostrils only the good warm smell of the sun on their bodies.

At home with his colt and mare, William Rysdyk fell to work with dogged energy. "That Dutchman is touched in the head," his neighbors said as they gaped over their fences, watching him toil and sweat for the lame mare and the overbig colt. They watched him make a foundation of stones on the slope of a hill, wondering why he piled the stones so high in front and so low against the hill. When he moved the sloping-roofed chicken shed and set it on the foundation, then they knew.

"It got to be high roofed for mare-mom now and for Hamble-tonian when he gets big," Rysdyk told the curious onlookers. "And if it got chicken lice, I end them," he said, pouring boiling water over lye ashes and brooming the walls with fierce pleasure.

As a crowning touch he thatched the roof for warmth in winter and coolness in summer. When the work was done he stood proud, as a brood-mare face and a young quizzical one looked out upon their master. "Is snug!" he said. "Rough-made but not leaky. By criminy! A little family can be happy here like anything!"

"Hmpf!" the neighbors snorted. "He looks more bull than colt." And behind the Dutchman's back and to his face, the colt became known as "Rysdyk's Big Bull."

The more they taunted, however, the more firmly the man believed in the greatness of his colt, and the steadier he trained him. Up before the stars faded, teaching him to whoa, leading him at the trot. Faster and faster each morning, until both man and colt grew hard-muscled and deep-lunged.

As for the mare, she seemed to grow younger with the months.

When anyone came near, both she and her colt would strike a trot for the pure excitement of speed.

Always late at night after chores were done, Rysdyk hied himself to the little hillside barn with old salt sacks for rub rags. There he would curry and groom until two coats shone glossy bright. Sometimes when he had finished rubbing Hambletonian's coat he stood back in awe, reluctant to run his rough fingertips across it for fear of snagging the satin.

With two creatures dependent on him, William Rysdyk's work had a new strength and purpose. Sleeves rolled, he faced each season like a giant refreshed—splitting logs, hauling, plowing as if he were made of iron. Peter Townsend's and Jonas Seely's acres began yielding more wheat, more rye, more corn. This pleased them so greatly they gave their hired hand a Jersey milch cow and a Holstein.

And each month the money-till in the teapot was opened and silver dollars tucked inside. Soon the debt would be paid. Soon the mare and colt would be William Rysdyk's. Only once did he dip into his savings. A pure white leather halter hanging from the ceiling in the general store seemed made for the colt.

"Maybe this I buy for the Fair, not knowing, yet knowing," he chuckled as he fastened it on Hambletonian.

On a clear September day, without any more thought, without any planning, he entered Hambletonian, now two years old, in the Orange County Fair. The whole idea came on him suddenly. He knew he owned the best two-year-old in the county; it was high time others knew.

When the time arrived for Rysdyk to bring out his colt, the judges shouted, "Make way! Make way!" And indeed the warning was needed. Men, women, children jumped back in alarm to escape the flying heels. Lead rein in hand, William Rysdyk ran up and

down showing his colt at the trot. He forgot he was at the Fair. He forgot everything in the rhythm of his colt's trot. Side by side they went, man and horse, evenly matched, not wanting to whoa. Not either of them.

It was the judge, cupping his hands to his mouth, bellowing his command, that called a halt. "Whoa!" he roared. *"First prize in the two-year-old stallion class to Hambletonian by Abdallah."*

The crowd stood stunned as the blue ribbon and the five-dollar premium went to William Rysdyk. Their mouths were open, their hands rigid at their sides. They could not applaud. When at last their tongues loosed, they said, "Oh—him," pointing to the colt. "The judge has been taken in by the fine white halter and the *man's* endurance. Does the ribbon stand for speed? No! Does it stand for style? Sakes, no! Not with only two other stallions in the competition."

And so the blue ribbon added little to the colt's fame. Not even in the eyes of his owner. William Rysdyk already knew his horse was best.

With the five-dollar premium he bought an old, dilapidated gig with a hub and two spokes missing. After seeing to its repair and building a box on it, he used it to deliver milk to the Erie Railroad for Mister Seely, Mister Townsend, and himself. The colt, frisky and green, trotted between the shafts.

"I get a color when I think it is you I drive to a milk wagon," William Rysdyk confided in him on their first trip. "But look once," he said to the pricked ears, "how it with us stands. Soon the old teapot gets heavy with silver. Soon is all fixed up with Mister Seely, and you I own. Outright! Then will you have it pleasant with me."

The third time out, Hambletonian looked as comfortable in harness as he did in halter. He was jogging down the main pike, full of play as a kitten, shaking his head and bugling to the morning. Behind him, in the box of the cart, the milk cans made a pleasant rattling.

Suddenly, halfway between Sugar Loaf and Chester town, he felt a few drops of rain on his nose. They were big drops. Big and far apart at first. Then a wind came up and the rain smalled and needled, pricking him, now on the back, now on the face.

He asked William Rysdyk to go. As plainly as it is given a horse to talk, he said, "Let's step! To the station to dump the milk cans. Then home! Home to the snug hillside barn, with hay wisping out of the rack."

"Yah, shure!" William Rysdyk answered the colt, for the rain dripped from his hat brim and now was running coldly down his neck. And the wind kept lifting his wet beard, slapping it across his face. "Yah, shure!" he agreed. "Is better we should go!"

And go they did. Like eels through water. The countryside swam past them. The pike was theirs. Beckoning to them, curling a finger at them. Then in a flash of lightning they saw a blur in the distance. A humpbacked blur crawling on the road, crawling like some beetle. Only bigger. Blacker. Blocking the pike.

"Over-catch it!" cried William Rysdyk, and Hambletonian bore down on the beetly thing. It was a gig! Shiny new, drawn by a high-stepping black. Rain sheeted over the blackness of it, over the black umbrella of the driver, over the black back of the horse.

Hambletonian wanted to be rid of it, to get around it, to kick rain in its face.

But the black thing was black in spirit, too. It hogged the center of the pike, lurching fearlessly toward the ditches on either side, the ditches deep and slippery with rain.

Now Hambletonian was gaining on the beetle, warning it with oncoming hoof beats. Unless it flew away, he was going to trot right over it, smashing its shiny shell. William Rysdyk's mouth went open to cry "Whoa!" But the word died on his lips. For to his left a farmer's lane came out, broadening to meet the road. Perhaps they could pass the black beetle there. Perhaps.

Now the colt saw it, too, now felt his right rein slacken, felt a tightening of his left, felt his head turning the way he wanted to go! The way was his! With twenty-foot strides he caught the black just as he hit the widened place in the road, then whipped around him, back onto the pike, the cart teetering wildly.

"Hurrah!" cried Rysdyk. "You done it!" And the milk cans rattled and applauded in the box.

In the midst of a hurrah William Rysdyk glanced back. The man jouncing under the umbrella was long-nosed Henry Spingler! At the self-same instant Mister Spingler caught as in a glare of light the dilapidated gig, the teetering milk cans, the beard strangely familiar, and the big-eared colt. His back stiffened. A chunk horse passing his black! A chunk horse a pacemaker for him!

He slapped the lines, lifted them, lifting the black's head,

yelling to him, yelling at him, roaring with the thunder.

"So big a noise from so little a man!" laughed William Rysdyk.

And now the black began to step, lengthening his stride, settling to business.

Hambletonian pounded on, his ears laced back, tormented by the cracking of Spingler's whip. Down the main street of Chester, past the inn, past the church, the bank, the postoffice, the general store they raced, the black still trailing. Bankers, printers, storekeepers came running out, bareheaded in the rain. The din was ear-splitting. Hoofs clattering. Milk cans clanking. Voices cheering, some for Rysdyk's Big Bull, and some for the black.

"By golly," exclaimed William Rysdyk, "the speed comes sooner as I think! A colt making challenge to Mister Spingler's horse!" A wild ecstasy poured through him as he felt the give and take between Hambletonian's mouth and his own hand. "Maybe his hips *is* higher as his shoulders? Maybe so. What else gives the pushing power? *What else?*"

For a full mile Main Street ran straight as a whiffletree, then turned sharply to the right along the Erie tracks to the station.

The road was wide enough for a good brush, wide enough for horses to go abreast, for horses to pass. But there was no passing. Hambletonian was mighty as the storm. He was a bolt of lightning, fearing nothing, driven by the thunder of his own speed. The black lumbered along behind, as if Mister Spingler were an anchor around his neck.

They were nearing the turn now and William Rysdyk took a quick glance over his shoulder. He saw Mister Spingler reach for the whip, saw him crack it across his horse's rump, saw at the same instant the wind whoosh under the umbrella and blow it inside out.

Hambletonian saw it, too. He made a shying jump, then caught his trot. But the black, frightened out of his wits, broke into a wild gallop, broke free of the shafts, and streaked for home. The gig, however, slurred on, making a beeline for a bed of canna lilies at the door of the station. It wound up there, very still, with one wheel off. And poking up very pertly between its spokes were canna lilies, red and yellow.

As William Rysdyk reined in, he looked back amazed. Mister Spingler, in top hat, was sitting in the flower bed, sitting quite upright in what was left of the gig. And in his hand he held, like a torch, the inside-out umbrella.

Mister Spingler Hurls a Challenge

Mister Spingler was not one to forget. At dusk that very evening he appeared in the doorway of William Rysdyk's cowshed. Behind him was the committee—John Doughty, Israel Toothill with dog-at-heel, and Mister Dandy, the driver, wearing a coat much less elegant.

"Ahem," coughed Mister Spingler.

Rysdyk was intent on milking his Holstein at the time, and the sound startled him so completely he almost upset his milkpail. He stumbled to his feet, remembering his manners.

"How make you it?" he asked the men politely.

Mister Spingler ignored the question. He inserted two fingers between the buttons of his waistcoat. "You may finish your milking," he said. "Then we would have a word with you."

Two more squirts and the pail was full. William Rysdyk now poured the steaming milk into a can, lowered it into a tank of water, and came over to the waiting men.

"We have come," Mister Spingler announced, "to see the colt. Be so good as to trot him out."

Slowly, puzzled, Rysdyk walked across the pasture lot to the barn, wondering what the men could want. Still more slowly he opened the door of the colt's stall, standing proudly to one side as the horse charged out like Messenger down the gangplank. With nostrils distended he sampled the air. Then he trotted across the grassy plot as if his legs had springs in them.

"Sic your sheep dog on him," Mister Spingler commanded Mister Toothill. "I'll wager *he* can make him break from that trot."

Israel Toothill made a hissing sound, and with a yelp the dog was off. Across the pasture he chased the colt, snapping and barking at his heels. But the colt danced neatly out of his way, never once shifting from his trot.

William Rysdyk broke out in a guffaw that made the blood rise in Mister Spingler's face. The little man spun around, turning his back on the sight. "You, Rysdyk!" he said, coming very close to him. "We've a challenge to propose to you."

As William Rysdyk's head went up in surprise, his beard brushed Mister Spingler's long bill nose.

The man stepped back in disgust. "We have come," he sniffed, rubbing his nose, "to propose for your beast a public trial at the Union Course on Long Island. This would give you an opportunity to show his speed. And *fairly*," he added, "with no umbrella to frighten his opponent."

Rysdyk steadied himself against the barn, looking at the faces of the men, from one to the other. The import of the words numbed him. The Union Course. Long Island. A public trial. Over the same mile Bishop's Hambletonian and Silvertail had trotted!

"Well?" Mister Spingler said sharply.

"Excuse, sir. It fuddles me. What say you again?"

Mister Spingler felt his colleagues' eyes on him. He pulled himself up, speaking deliberately. "Perhaps you are afraid. Afraid your horse lacks the stamina."

"Him?" William Rysdyk exploded. "Why, he can trot out quicker as anything, and he still got some power over. By golly, look on him now."

Mister Spingler turned around to look. It was true. The colt with the dog yapping at his heels seemed as fresh as when he had pranced out of his stall.

"Please to call up your dog, sir," William Rysdyk said, surprised at his own boldness.

When the dog came in, panting and slavering, John Doughty and Israel Toothill and Mister Dandy broke into the talk, anxious to get the matter settled. Their sentences came quick and staccato.

"The match will come off Tuesday next."

"Sharp at three."

"Trotting against your colt will be his half brother—Abdallah Chief, owned by Mister Roe."

"First The Chief will trot the mile. Then your horse."

"The better time wins."

"As to the matter of finances," the banker said, "the committee will pay the costs of shipping your colt over the Erie, and Mister Seely has donated the use of his skeleton wagon, the same one Silvertail drew over the same course."

Now everything was said. A strained silence followed, broken only by the panting of the sheep dog.

Mister Spingler tapped his boot, vexed at the delay. "Do you or do you not wish to match him?"

"That I know not, sir. Abdallah Chief—him I have seen. He is over the four years, leaned from the racing. Hambletonian, he is yet a round-barreled colt, and only three times in the harness."

"Very well, if you have no confidence..."

William Rysdyk gave a look of contempt. "Who said it we would not go? We got to!" he announced, pride rising in him.

The banker pulled a notebook and a gold pencil from the tail of his coat. "Now then, how do you spell your horse's name?"

The Dutchman began—slowly, haltingly. "Hah, ah, em, bay, el, ay, tay, oh, en, ee, ah, en."

Mister Spingler smiled down his nose. "Gentlemen," he said, "the oaf has named the colt after our hero, Alexander Hamilton, yet he knows not how to spell the name."

A deep flush came over William Rysdyk's face. How could he explain to the men that he had named his horse for Hambletonian, the hero of his childhood? He would not try.

The driver laughed. "Why not call him Rysdyk's Big Bull? It will add flavor to the notices. Rysdyk's Big Bull against The Chief."

Match Against Time

Early on the morning of the match, William Rysdyk stepped into Tiffany's, a new jewelry store in New York City.

"A timekeeper I would want to buy," he said timidly to the spruce gentleman who leaned across the showcase. "To click it on when my colt strikes off on the Union Course. What for time-keepers have you?"

The gentleman opened a narrow drawer behind him and took out a shiny watch on a long cord. "Of course, you know how it works," he said, "but I should like to make certain it is in perfect order." Turning the face toward William Rysdyk, he clicked the pin. He let the seconds run, sixty of them, and clicked it again. Then he placed the watch in his customer's hand, saying, "In perfect condition!" Thus in his quiet, thoughtful way the jeweler had shown a frightened stranger in New York how to work a stopwatch.

He smiled as he held open the door. "Remember, time waits for neither man nor horse."

"Is true!" William Rysdyk nodded heartily. He walked away, smiling to himself. "That Mr. Tiffany will make a go of it, I betcha."

His smile died on his lips. A light rain was falling. "Ach, the track!" he cried, clapping his hands to his head. "It goes sticky on me." He was in a frenzy to get there, as if he could mop it up singlehanded.

But when he did get there, the rain was falling in a steady curtain. There was nothing to do but watch it out the window of Hambletonian's stall. Desolate, he threw a blanket on the straw and lay down, inviting Hambletonian to join him. Together, man and colt slept, and the rain quieted and stopped, and the wind came up and blew cold.

And as they slept, the first spectators began coming to the course, spreading handkerchiefs and butcher's paper over the damp seats. Jonas Seely left his group in the stands to look in on his hired man.

"Ho there, man! Awake! The hour is at hand!"

65

William Rysdyk scrambled to his feet and looked up at the sky. "The weather strikes around. God lets go the pump handle, eh?"

"Aye, but a gale blows now. However, it takes more than wind and storm to keep true sportsmen away. Naturally, the assemblage is not so great as it was for the race between Fashion and Peytona or for Fashion and Boston, but what it lacks in numbers it makes up in quality."

"So?"

"Aye," Mister Seely nodded. "Already I have spotted Oliver Holmes, Ralph Emerson, and His Honor, Ambrose T. Kingsland, Mayor of New York."

William Rysdyk came out of the stall and looked at the stands. His mouth went dry. Top hats and poke bonnets were thick as flies in a blacksmith shop, and in the centerfield was a higgledy-piggledy conglomeration of carts and gigs and chariots and landaus and phaetons and broughams. He had never seen so many turnouts. He looked helplessly at Mister Seely.

"Excuse, sir, Hambletonian and me—is maybe better we tail it from here. We could home be already by morning."

"Come, come, man. The colt will give you confidence. The gentleman yonder," he indicated the direction with a slight lift of his elbow, "the one smoking the big cigar, is Mister Roe, owner

of Abdallah Chief."

William Rysdyk took one look at the man, standing big and calm, watching while his hired help wheeled out one of the new sulkies. "Ach, to be at home," thought Rysdyk. Digging ditches. Sacking onions. Splitting wood. Anything. If only he had known! Now it was too late. He looked down at the patches on his knees, at his stable boots.

The crowd was growing. Mister Seely pulled out his watch. "Half after two," he said. "Note Mister Roe now. He is warming up The Chief. He trots the mile at three on the hour. Then immediately afterward comes your turn."

With hands cold and trembling Rysdyk began harnessing— slipping the breast collar over Hambletonian's neck, his tail through the crupper, setting the pad on his back, buckling the bellyband. He felt to see if the collar and bridle fitted comfortably.

As his hands touched the colt, he asked himself, "What matters it if my breeches is rough and patched? Hambletonian's coat is satin, without flaw, his hoofs shining from beeswax. The crowd— they come for him, not me."

Hambletonian was restive, sensing the tension in the air. Today there was no rattle of milk cans. Today was different. And the wind! Already it distended his nostrils, lifted his mane, excited him.

The bugles and drums! The wind had affected them, too. Quavered the notes, carried them high on wind shoulders.

Now Mister Roe was driving Abdallah Chief out on the track. How slim and sleek The Chief! How wiry from his racing! The spectators liked him. Their cheers left no doubt.

"The cheers care I not for!" Rysdyk took out his stopwatch. "What matters is the time."

"Go!" came the word. And The Chief went, hugging the rail, taking advantage of the distance saved. William Rysdyk's eyes darted ahead to the quarter pole, waiting for the horse to pass. As he whipped by, the new watch said forty-four seconds!

The assemblage was on its feet. Abdallah Chief was going the pace they expected. One twenty-nine at the half. Now his pace was increasing. Two-eleven and a half at the three-quarter pole. Faster down the stretch! He was passing the wire now—two minutes, fifty-five and a half seconds at the finish.

The time was good in the gale, the crowd satisfied with its choice. Better marks had been made, they told each other. Flora Temple had done the same distance in less time. So had Lady Suffolk. But then the track had been fast and the wind still. The performance of The Chief was good. Mister Roe drove him back to his stall, looking mightily pleased. The Chief, however, seemed tired on his legs, blowing as if his lungs were fit to burst.

Again the bugle shrilling in the wind. But if it had been no louder than a penny whistle it would have pierced William Rysdyk's ears. And now the roll of the drums. The bugle and the drums were inside him, in his stomach, his lungs, his heart.

Now it was! Now the time had come! He mounted Silvertail's big wagon, set his feet against the dashboard, braced himself. He took the reins. He cradled the stop watch in his palm. To his surprise his hand held steady and it was the crowd that fluttered.

68

What if their cheers were few and raveling away in laughter? His eyes and ears were not for them. He was seeing between the ears of his colt, seeing the wet, gummy mile, waiting for the word.

"Go!" it came like a knifeblade sharpened on the wind. The colt and the watch clicked off in unison. And suddenly William Rysdyk knew the watch was his opponent. Not The Chief, but the live little thing in his hand. The little gold thing with a white face and little fine wires inside. She was his opponent.

The sticky track was on her side, cupping at the colt's feet, sucking at them, holding them back. The high wind was on her side, blowing pieces of paper in Hambletonian's face. The white picket fence was on her side. The colt had never seen such a high fence before. He shied from it. No hugging the rail to save precious yards and Time.

The seconds were ticking themselves off, ticking away all safe and secure, away from the wind, away from the fence, away from the cuppy track. Time was his match! Time grinning up at him from the white face with nervous little hands.

In front of him the satin haunches, the driving legs punching out, clawing to grip the track, clawing and slipping. On the first turn the wagon began to skid. Rysdyk slowed the piston legs, slowed them. Even the turns were on the watch's side.

Forty-one seconds at the quarter pole. The colt was a match for Time! Now for a half mile without any turns. And the colt saw it, going like a steam engine, his tail the black smoke. Now the wind was a prodding stick, pricking inside his nose, pricking along his chest, his barrel, his legs, lifting his forelock, his mane. Rushing at him on all sides, jangling in his ears, spurring him.

One twenty-three at the half! William Rysdyk felt pride rising with the wind. His colt was speed, harnessed speed.

Tears blurred his eyes. He blinked them fiercely away. Two-seven and a half at the third quarter. The horse and Time were flying together, beat for beat, second for second.

Now one more turn. The wagon sluing again on the wet clay, teetering on two wheels! William Rysdyk leaned far out to hold it on the track, pushing with his body, his feet, holding his breath in anguish as two iron tires spun free of the earth in a singing whine.

"Mein Gott!" Too late to slow down. He leaned harder, the breath hurting in his lungs. And then, "Danke Gott!" To his relief he felt the wagon down, felt the jolt and the relief all in one.

And now for the brush down the stretch! Rysdyk straining, pushing forward, sitting bird-light in the seat, longing to trot alongside the colt, yoked to him, somehow worthy of him.

The white face in his hand. Two minutes, forty-eight and a half seconds as they crossed the finish line. Hambletonian had won! His time was better than The Chief's! Seven seconds better!

The crowd was finding its voice, waving handkerchiefs and muffs big as bedpillows. The crowd was a flag of many colors, flung on the wind, now rippling in, closing in on Hambletonian. And the judge was jumping down from his perch, raising his hand, shouting with the throng.

"Huzzah for Rysdyk's Big Bull! Huzzah for Rysdyk's Big Bull!"

Suddenly William Rysdyk's voice burst into a shout, lustier than any other: "Hurrah for Rysdyk's Big Bull!"

The "bull" himself stood shining with sweat, his ears laced back, not because he was displeased but because he was the son of Old Abdallah.

"Excuse, please." William Rysdyk tried to speak out above the applause. "The colt he must not stand in the wind. I must now put his blanket on and walk him out." But his voice was lost in the huzzahs.

70

Till Seeing

Top hats, handkerchiefs, muffs were still waving over the Union Course as William Rysdyk drove off. The performance of the untried colt had first stunned and thrilled the spectators; then a wondering set in. What could Rysdyk's Big Bull have done with training? With a skilled driver? On a fast track? On a windless day? What could he have done hooked to a light sulky instead of a cumbrous wagon?

And now what could he, as a sire, do to improve the speed and stamina of the American trotter? The question flew from mouth to mouth during the weeks that followed the Union Course race. And more than one man stood ready to answer it. Stock-breeders, dirt farmers, dairymen, men cooped up in office buildings, men from near, men from far—all wanted to buy the colt. Two gentlemen journeyed up from Virginia to bid ten thousand dollars for him. At first their offers were spoken low, in quiet confidence. Then the bidding picked up. Soon offers and voices were raised in impatience.

"Sh! Don't speak it out so loud," William Rysdyk said, motioning toward Hambletonian. "He don't like it. Already I know him since he was eating off his mare-mom. No, by criminy! Hambletonian and me—we wouldn't going to separate now. There's *nobody* could buy him."

In the years that followed, many horsemen brought their mares to Hambletonian to be bred and thus improve their trotting stock. One was Ulysses S. Grant, President of the United States. It was the President's approval that helped carry the name of Hambletonian throughout the world.

And it was the President who noted a unique characteristic in Hambletonian's colts: their hips stood higher than their withers. He gave a name to this conformation. The "trotting pitch" he called it. And what Israel Toothill and his august committee had once laughed at, horsemen now began seeking.

With each year Hambletonian's fame grew and spread. At one Orange County Fair, while a vast throng sent up cheers and clamorings, Hambletonian and nine of his big-going sons trotted around a giant oak tree in the centerfield.

"Hero of Orange County! King of Sires! Father of the Turf!" they shouted now. And the name "Rysdyk's Big Bull" buried itself in the dust of the past.

Whether his colts trotted to wagon, to sulky or under saddle, they set new marks for speed. Good as these marks were, his grand-colts kicked their heels at them, setting records of their own.

The line strengthened as it lengthened! Each new generation clipped off seconds until Hambletonian became the most famous stallion in all America.

Year on year at the county fairs, old and young would stop in admiration when William Rysdyk drove him into the grounds. And year on year the stallion would win blue ribbons with gold lettering that said, "Best stallion in his class." He won silver cups, too, and a sterling silver tea set because of all stallions he was judged best.

Of course, William Rysdyk had no more use for silver cups and tea sets than for water in his hat, but he accepted them all as custodian for Hambletonian. And often on moon-bright nights he would steal out to the barn with lye ashes and rag to polish them. "Foolish, eh?" he would chortle as he rubbed. "Yah, foolish but not caring. In some other world maybe his thirst gets gentler and out of tea cups he drinks."

In time William Rysdyk's beard turned white, and white hairs too grew around Hambletonian's muzzle. And still the horse was above price. As the man and the stallion grew old together, they looked upon each other with their hearts as well as their eyes.

In the spring of 1870 Rysdyk fell ill, and it became the custom of young James, man-grown now, to look in on the elderly Dutchman who had been like an uncle to him. One clear, starlit evening, Rysdyk welcomed his visitor with a special urgency. James did not take time to lay aside his coat nor to remove the newspaper from his pocket. He knelt beside the bed, looking into the bearded face, into eyes that once had scolded him when he left his playthings about. Now the eyes pleaded.

—After an early lithograph by Currier & Ives

"Tonight there is just two wishes I could maybe want to wish." Rysdyk's breath came short but a smile played about his lips. "Can you once to boost up on me so out my window Hambletonian I could see?"

With awkward but gentle hands the young man propped the pillows behind the hired man's back. Then he threw wide the shutters, saying, "I will go out now and lead your horse in front of the window."

Turning to go, something caused James to glance out-of-doors. To his wonderment he saw the stallion footing his way slowly and majestically toward the open window. Head upraised, ears pricked forward like trumpets, he came closer, step by step. He may only have been harkening to the cry of a hawk thin on the wind, but perchance he heard a beloved voice calling. As his head reached the window, the voice spoke only two words. "Till seeing," it said, "till seeing."

At sound of the familiar singsong the stallion began to quiver, and suddenly in a long trembling neigh of remembrances added his voice to One Man's.

With a sigh of satisfaction William Rysdyk sank back among the pillows. "When deep sleep comes to him," he whispered to the Seely boy, "he has it on the green hillside with a name marker? Yah? In my will we make it up so? Yah?"

The young man nodded.

And so it was.

It is not given to horses to write wills. But some there are who say Hambletonian's descendants are his testament.

And some say Hambletonian wrote his will in music—American music, the tap-tap, tap-tap ringing of hoofbeats.

HEAD STUDY
BY GEORGE FORD MORRIS

The Great Sire

HIS NAME WAS HAMBLETONIAN 10 in Wallace's Trotting Register Volume I, but in horse circles he is always Rysdyk's Hambletonian. He outlived his master by six years and those were spent under the watchful eye of a neighbor, Guy Miller. He would have pleased William Rysdyk in all things.

Daily, with the exception of Sundays, Miller drove Hambletonian hitched to the old skeleton wagon* on the main pike—now Hambletonian Avenue—to Chester. It was only a cinder lane then, but wide enough to challenge all comers to a fast brush.

* A stripped-down four-wheel buggy or wagon.

"Whenever the old stallion felt good," Miller confessed, "he made rushes so fast they fairly frightened me, and I was glad to have him settle down and drop back to a slower gait."

Both before and after these morning jaunts, Harmon Showers—a little cherry-brown man who was part Indian and part black—groomed the stallion's coat, cleaned out his hoofs, and tended his every need. Without ever saying so, he silently worshiped Hambletonian as if he sensed that the stallion was marked for immortality.

Few horses in history have been cared for as lovingly in their last years as Hambletonian. His sire, Old Abdallah, with the royal blood of Imported Messenger in his veins, fell into the hands of a fish peddler. Detesting the smell of fish, he kicked the cart to pieces, spewing flounder and cod in every direction. The fishmonger,

His skeleton wagon and Hambletonian were a familiar sight on the road to Che

slipping and scrambling over his dead fish, was so enraged he abandoned Old Abdallah on the spot, which happened to be Grave's End Beach on Long Island.

An artist who heard about the incident was intrigued by the picture in his mind: a beachcomber of a stallion, browsing on tufts of sea grass against a white-capped sea and sky. But by the time he found his subject, Old Abdallah was trapped in a roofless shed, standing knee-deep in sand, his coat so long and woolly he looked more buffalo than horse. As the artist went after help to get the horse free, buzzards were already circling the spot. Old Abdallah died alone.

In contrast Hambletonian was curried and cared for to the end of his life, which came quite suddenly on a blustery March day in

Hambletonian 10, greatest foundation sire of the Standard-bred trotter

PORTRAIT BY GEORGE FORD MORRIS

1876. He was nearly twenty-eight at the time, an ancient in man-years, but sound and fit almost to the last.

Farmers and their families, storekeepers and their clerks, all the residents of Orange County felt a deep sense of loss. They would miss the familiar sight and the sound of Hambletonian's clippity-trot to Chester town.

Like kings of old, the Hero of Sugar Loaf—as the *Times Herald* called him—was lowered into a specially built box, large enough to hold all his worldly goods: his blanket and hoods, his halter and harness, even his currycomb and dandy brush.

With schools and businesses closed in Hambletonian's honor, hundreds of children and grownups marched past his bier and later peered into his stall hoping to find one of his castoff shoes, or at least a hair from his mane or tail.

In a plot near the stable, under a wild cherry tree where he had liked to scratch against the bark, Hambletonian was buried. The day was bleak and stormy, and the sough of the wind seemed to echo the words of Jonas Seely, a very old man now, who leaned on his son's shoulder as he spoke.

"Gentle peace to him that sleeps in the mystery of death
   but lives in the heartbeats and hoofbeats of his sons."

For six years Hambletonian's grave was marked only by a small white stone. During those years Guy Miller acquired two of Hambletonian's sons, founded his Greycourt Farm, and felt an overwhelming gratitude to Hambletonian. He, together with other breeders, wanted to build a fitting monument to the grand ancestor of their horses. Diligently they went to work with letters and personal calls until dollars came in by the ones and hundreds. Within a year the plans and fund grew large enough to erect an obelisk of red Ozark granite. It was inscribed to

HAMBLETONIAN
The Great Progenitor of Trotters
Born May 5, 1849
Died March 27, 1876

On winter days the towering shaft seems to stab the deep of the sky and can be seen for miles and miles. In summer the tip is lost among the leaves of a giant maple that has crowded out the wild cherry tree.

Barely a mile away, on what is now the old Bull farm, lies William Rysdyk, the Dutch farmhand whose belief in one horse is still making history.

HOW THE TROTTING RACES STARTED

In England, in the century before Hambletonian, horse racing was the sport of kings. Running horses, as they were called, raced for purse* and glory at such famous courses as Newmarket and Epsom Downs. But the trotters, unpampered, worked instead of raced. They were the stout-bodied coach horses that splashed their way as fast as possible through the mud and mire of the bad roads.

At the same time, in America, the puritanical settlers of the Northeast felt that racing for big purses attracted "scalawags and rowdies." So in 1802 they banned the sport entirely and closed the few tracks in existence.

These same critics, however, saw nothing wrong with a skilled driver behind a quick trotter overtaking a neighbor with a trappy horse and challenging him to a fast brush—merely to test their horses. Seldom did any money change hands; it was sport for sport's sake. Everyone did it—parson or blacksmith, banker or farmer—on the way to Saturday market or Sunday meeting. A friendly brush, going or coming, added yeast to the day.

Crisp winter weather increased the fun. Drivers, buttoned-up and mufflered, found snow-packed roads even better for brushing. But winter or summer, impromptu races became so widespread that pedestrians had to leap to safety to avoid hoofs and wheels.

As a life-saving measure the city fathers blocked off certain streets for speedsters—Third Avenue and Harlem Lane in New York City and Jamaica Road on Long Island. These became the fashionable speedways that rivaled in excitement today's Kentucky Derby or the Hambletonian Stake.

---

* Literally there was a purse ... filled with gold coins. It was hung on the wire at the finish post. The winning jockey, with his retinue, would ride back to collect the purse and carry it in triumph before the spectators.

And then, twenty-five years after the tracks had closed down, they were reopened, but with an interesting restriction. Because gallopers could go a few seconds faster than trotters, and this might lead to gambling, the gallopers were still banned but the trotters were in! Thus religion was a boon to the development of a new breed, unique to America ... the Standardbred.

The first official trotting races were not to wagon or sulky, but under saddle. The style of riding would be startling today. Jockeys of all sizes and shapes sat stiff as pikestaffs, never crouching over the horse's neck, not even when bowling down the homestretch.

New York trotters in a heated skirmish in the snow

SKETCH BY T. WORTH FOR CURRIER & IVES, YALE UNIVERSITY ART GALLERY

The oldest painting of a trotting race—not in harness, but under saddle

Lady Suffolk, the old grey mare of Long Island, was the spectacular trotter of the 1840s, once carrying a rider weighing more than 180 pounds! She took part in 162 races, and placed in all but nine.

The Lady reached the peak of her career the year that William Rysdyk came upon an awkward newborn foal and saw in him Messenger charging down the gangplank. Lady Suffolk, too, owed her power and her pure trotting action to their common thoroughbred ancestor.

OLD AB'S NAMESAKE

The remarkable span of Lady Suffolk's career prodded men to dream. What could be done to encourage the breeding of good trotting horses?

84

Lady Suffolk, the old grey mare of Long Island, raced until she was 20

Soon the words *pedigree* and *rootstock* were debated in shed and stable, kitchen and drawingroom. Wherever horsemen gathered they began diagramming, on scraps of paper or in ledger books, the family tree of "natural lot trotters," including of course Rysdyk's young stallion, Hambletonian. What they discovered was that on his dam's side as well as his sire's, he traced straight back to Imported Messenger.

Word flew like the March wind. From miles away, mares of fine breeding and of ordinary breeding were sent to Hambletonian so that his blood could purify that of future generations. In time, the list of his sons and daughters began to read like the begets and the begats of the Bible.

Among Hambletonian's first and most famous sons was Abdallah 15, known also as Alexander's Abdallah. The life of this namesake of Old Abdallah was a drama of coincidences. His dam,

85

TROTTING STALLION

HAMBLETONIAN,

WILL STAND FOR A LIMITED NUMBER OF MARES,

At the stable of **WM. M. RYSDYK**, in Chester, from the first day of **April** to the first day of **August**.

$25 THE SEASON, & $35 TO INSURE A MARE WITH FOAL.

Season money due the first day of August next, and insurance money due on the first day of March, 1856

Rare poster of Rysdyk's Hambletonian standing at Chester, New York

Katy Darling, had broken her ankle on the Seventh Avenue Speedway in almost the exact spot where the Kent mare suffered her accident. Perhaps in nostalgic memory, William Rysdyk had permitted the limping Katy to be bred to Hambletonian.

In September of 1852 her colt, a reddish bay with Abdallah's fiery temper and his long peaked ears, was born. He was finally purchased—after a series of exhibitions and a series of owners—by R. A. Alexander of Kentucky, who promptly entered him in Wallace's Register as both Alexander's Abdallah and Abdallah 15.

For the next years Alexander's Abdallah lived an idyllic existence in the lushness of the Blue Grass country, never wearing shoes, frisking barefoot the day long.

Then came the War Between the States and his world collapsed. A guerilla raider stole him from his Blue Grass paradise and rode him fifty miles barefoot with Federal troops pounding and firing in pursuit. The race led over bad roads and none at all and through icy streams until his feet were torn and bleeding. Approaching the Ohio border, the raider stole a fresh horse and abandoned Abdallah to die alone.

Like Old Ab he suffered a needless and tragic death. But in his brief lifetime he had sired a family of champions, among them the spitfire, Goldsmith Maid, who broke world trotting records seven times. As Queen of the Turf she traveled in her private railway car, setting records for speed and attendance wherever she went.

Goldsmith Maid in a brush home with American Girl, July 4, 1868

CURRIER & IVES PRINT, YALE UNIVERSITY ART GALLERY

JUNIOR? ACH, NO!

Before Goldsmith Maid brought fame to her sire and grandsire, Hambletonian had fathered three other colts who became legends in harness history: Volunteer, George Wilkes, and Dexter.

Volunteer, of all his sons, was the most elegant both in conformation and bearing. His first owner, a Presbyterian deacon, Joseph Hetzel, had named him Hambletonian, Jr. Rysdyk viewed with jealousy this "Junior" title. It irked him like a nettle in his shirt, but he kept his feelings to himself—that is, until the man Hetzel accepted a dare to race "Junior" in the speed class at the Orange County Fair. The deacon, who gloried in a lively contest, not only welcomed the challenge but asked and got permission from the judges to start his entry behind all the others. For half the distance he held Hambletonian, Jr. far back and on the outside of the pack. Then he jiggled the bit, clucked like a mother hen, and the young

Volunteer, blue ribbon winner and speed sire

trotter swept past the field, one by one, to lead the way home by seven seconds with speed to spare.

After the race, Alden Goldsmith from Kentucky stepped up and bought the stallion to be shipped to his breeding establishment at Walnut Grove. This was too much to bear! Rysdyk's Dutch ire exploded. The name Hambletonian, Jr. *had* to be changed to avoid any confusion in the minds of the public. Goldsmith understood Rysdyk's feelings, and he chose the name Volunteer in deference to President Lincoln, who was calling up volunteers for the army.

Meanwhile the thrill of the come-from-behind race had taken the fancy of the whole country. "Game as Volunteer" became a catch phrase applied to every demonstration of courage—to children who obediently swallowed their castor oil, or to soldiers going into battle.

The number of Volunteer's colts was limited, but the prowess of his son St. Julien will long be remembered. St. Julien established three world records in one year at the ripe age of nine.

THE LITTLEST ORPHAN

In the order of time, George Wilkes is third among the great sons of Hambletonian, but in establishing a tribe of powerful trotters he stands first.

His is a Cinderella story. His mother, Dolly Spanker, was a trappy roadster owned by a New York grocer named Harry Felter. He drove Dolly in his business and in impromptu brushes on Third Avenue. Invariably Dolly was the winner. But she had a habit of purposely swishing her tail over the reins and pressing them to her buttocks so that Felter was helpless to guide her where *he* wanted to go. This so annoyed the man that he had her tail docked.

The effect of the operation was near paralysis and her trotting days were over. She was promptly sent to Hambletonian to be bred and then turned out in a pasture to fend for herself.

The following spring she was found under a tree, dead, with a puny little newborn trying to nudge her to life. A motherly woman in the Felter household, touched by the helplessness of the orphaned foal, consulted her doctor book and fed the tiny creature the same formula prescribed for a motherless baby—fresh cow's milk sweetened with a spoon of sugar and an eye-dropper of bourbon.

The colt flourished under the unlikely name of Robert Fillingham. What he lacked in size he made up in the lusty voice for his bottle and a kind of shining pocket-edition beauty. He was a sleek seal brown with one hind ankle white; and instead of the Abdallah look of coarseness he had inherited the Messenger mien of the Thoroughbred—ears small and busy, eyes large and eager—and he was evenly made, not low over the withers and high over the rump.

In spite of the colt's robust spirit, Felter wasn't pleased with his small size, so he sold him to Eph Simmons, a New York sportsman. In his very first race, Robert Fillingham showed his heels to two famous veterans of the track. And in his second start he made history by defeating the heavily favored Ethan Allen. The *Spirit of the Times* wrote in such glowing terms of the promise of the little stallion that Simmons renamed him George Wilkes in honor of the magazine's publisher.

What intrigued everyone—Simmons and spectators alike—was the unique gait of the young George Wilkes. He stepped along with a kind of skimming, swimming motion that journalists called "the duck stroke."

After a brilliant but punishing career of eleven seasons, George Wilkes was retired to the Blue Grass region of Kentucky where he

George Wilkes showing the way in the homestretch, 1869

also scored a brilliant success. Among his renowned sons were Bourbon Wilkes, Baron Wilkes, Brown Wilkes, Kentucky Wilkes, Wilkes Boy and Alcyone. An editorial in the *Times* declared: "No horse ever did so much for a state as George Wilkes, the little orphan with the duck paddle, did for Kentucky."

THE FLEET ONE

The fleetest son of Hambletonian was a splashily-marked brown gelding named Dexter. He defeated George Wilkes and all the best horses of his day to become the first world champion of the Hambletonian family. His record stunned every trotting horse fancier except one, William Rysdyk. The most surprised person was Jonathan Hawkins, his breeder, who had sold him as a weanling.

Could Hawkins have rejected the brown colt with the blazed face and the four white feet because he was "chock full of fire and and deviltry?" Or was he haunted by the old superstition:

91

Dexter, in slashing stride, proudly driven by President U.S. Grant

> One white foot, buy him;
> Two white feet, try him;
> Three white feet, sell him to your foes;
> Four white feet, feed him to the crows.

Dexter lost no time in exploding the myth. In his first season of racing he won four times in thirteen days, his white feet blurring down the stretch like the wings of a hummingbird.

England and France questioned whether any horse could travel at his speed either under saddle or to sulky, but there were too many witnesses and official timers to dispute his records.

On August 14, 1867, over the new Buffalo Driving Park Course, Dexter, in a race against time, trotted the mile in 2:17¼ to beat all records.

With the spectators still roaring and tossing their hats into the air, the distinguished Robert Bonner of Tarrytown mounted the judges' stand, waved for silence, and announced that he had just purchased the hero of the hour.

Mr. Bonner was a man apart. A financier, he was a churchman first. He considered racing for money a vice, believing the only way a man should test the mettle of his horse was on the open road. Besides, he believed that Dexter's record 2:17¼ was the absolute limit of trotting speed, quite beyond the power of any horse to equal.

Newspapers agreed. Front page stories carried pictures of the fleet-footed, white-footed horse in action. Soon the name Dexter appeared on skates and sleds, bicycles, hobby horses, and gilded weather vanes which are still spinning with the wind on barns and public buildings coast to coast.

On daily airings for over twenty years Robert Bonner, either alone or with a friend, enjoyed the sport of driving Dexter from his

Antique weather vane of Dexter, now a collector's item

93

stable on 27th Street to Prospect Park, engaging in little private brushes with any challenger whose hoofbeats came up from behind —where they always remained. Bonner's greatest compliment to a friend was to turn over the reins to him. General Ulysses S. Grant, in top hat and military bearing, was often honored.

HAMBLETONIAN'S MEADOW

It was Dexter who gave Hambletonian his world reputation as a sire of speed. But Dexter was by no means the last. Hambletonian's colts and grandcolts went on at a dizzying trot, slivering off the seconds until the year 1939, when Greyhound, with seven crosses of his blood to Hambletonian, shattered all records by trotting the mile in 1:55¼.

In all languages the reaction was *incredible.* An Italian horse owner who was eager to match his European champion, Muscletone, against Greyhound, traveled to the United States, took one look at the grey ghost flying along in a morning workout, and sailed for home—defeated without a contest.

Yet Greyhound, like Dexter, was born under a cloud of prejudice. Because of his grey color, he was gelded as a yearling, sold at a pittance, and his dam Elizabeth given away almost as a discard. Again, like Dexter, Greyhound defused an old myth:

> For speed choose a brown or a bay
> But never, no never, a grey!

While Greyhound was winning his early matches, W. Sanford Durland of Chester pondered on the source of his greatness. He wanted to show his appreciation to One Man's Horse who, through his blood, had created this champion of champions. But what fur-

*The great
Greyhound's
world record mile
of 1:55¼ held
for 30 years*

HEAD STUDY BY GEORGE FORD MORRIS

ther tribute could anyone pay? The towering marker on Hamble-tonian Avenue still stabbed the sky with as much beauty as ever. Perhaps something smaller would stir deeper thoughts in men's minds. What about Hambletonian's birthplace? Was the pleasant meadow still there, on the old Jonas Seely place? And what of the giant oaks? Were they still sheltering the spot where the Kent mare had dropped her foal?

On an Indian summer day in 1934, Mr. Durland traveled to the old Seely place, now the Banker Farm. He found the meadow untouched, and a lone surviving oak, a patriarch of trees, still growing and casting its acorns. And he found a boulder seemingly made for a commemorative marker to the patriarch of trotters.

The following August, the day after Greyhound had won the tenth Hambletonian Stake at Good Time Park in Goshen, a large and illustrious group of harness horse enthusiasts ventured through a cornfield and across a cow pasture to the foaling place. Among them was Miss Carrie Houston, the great-great-granddaughter of Jonas Seely.

When the buzz of talk quieted, J. J. Mooney, president of the Hambletonian Society, took his place beside the boulder, which was almost hidden by a plaid blanket once worn by Hambletonian.

"Friends!" He spoke in a clear voice that carried to the fringe of the gathering. "Every nook and corner of the world is noted for something. Some places produce precious gems, others are rich in gushing oil or beds of coal. All are God's gifts to man. Of his gifts, none has ever approached the horse. From ancient times it has been man and his horse: Alexander the Great and his Bucephalus, George Washington and his Nelson, Napoleon and his Marengo, Lord Wellington and his Copenhagen, Sheridan and his Rienzi,

An ancient oak still shelters the pasture where Hambletonian was foaled

96

Robert E. Lee and his Traveler, Stonewall Jackson and his Little Sorrell, and William Rysdyk and his Hambletonian. The last has given riches not only to our generation, but to generations to come."

Then a smiling Miss Carrie unveiled the handsome bronze tablet:

HAMBLETONIAN 10
Father of the Trotting Horse
Foaled On This Spot
May 5, 1849
Erected by His Admirers
August 15, 1935

It marks the spot where William Rysdyk came upon the Kent mare and a colt which he unhesitatingly named Hamble-tonian.

JUBILEE

And the accolades have never stopped. On May 5, 1949 all of Orange County turned out to celebrate the hundredth birthday of their foremost equine citizen, Hambletonian. Trotting fans from coast to coast had been invited, and many came dressed in nineteenth century garb.

It was a glory of a day, with four bands tootling and thumping, and trotting teams and singles in parade-step, and drivers wearing top hats or straws, and a mare-in-hand with a leggy foal tagging at heel, and a white-bearded farmhand who looked for all the world like William Rysdyk. It was the biggest parade in Chester's history, and not a car in sight!

Guy Miller's son, Richard, was the popular raconteur of the occasion, sharing the mementos and memories his father had handed down. "Our hero of Chester," he said, "may not have been a great beauty, but he had something besides looks. He had character, and we'll never see his like again."

Imported Messenger introduced the road-gait action into America

The birthday celebration proved such a rousing success that the younger citizens planned another for 1974, the one hundred twenty-fifth anniversary of Hambletonian's birth. This time it was to be called Hambletonian Day.

As the day neared, everybody pitched in. The 4-H'ers of Sugar Loaf made it their project to prune and whack and haul away the underbrush and overhang from the path that visitors would have to take from Hambletonian Road to the foaling meadow. And they built little bridges across the muddy spots. And they rubbed and polished the marker until the letters gleamed. Then on Hambletonian Day they placed a basket of spring flowers before the plaque and unfurled the 4-H flag and the American flag, placing one on

Mambrino from whom Hambletonian inherited his space-devouring stride

either side. They were proud and ready.

The festivities were marked by a trek from the foaling spot at Sugar Loaf to the granite monument at Chester and on to Historic Track at Goshen where Rysdyk's colt was first exhibited as a weanling. On this day races were held, with Hambletonian's descendants winging around the track, four-square and strong.

This holiday, too, was so filled with fun and fervor that when America later celebrated its Bicentennial, which historic character did Orange County choose to honor? Why, Rysdyk's Hambletonian, of course. Who else?

"In celebrating these anniversaries," Philip Pines, of the Hall of Fame of the Trotter, points out, "we are also honoring Hambletonian's illustrious ancestors and offspring."

In the time capsule of history they will all have their niche, but it is the ugly duckling of Sugar Loaf who wears the crown.

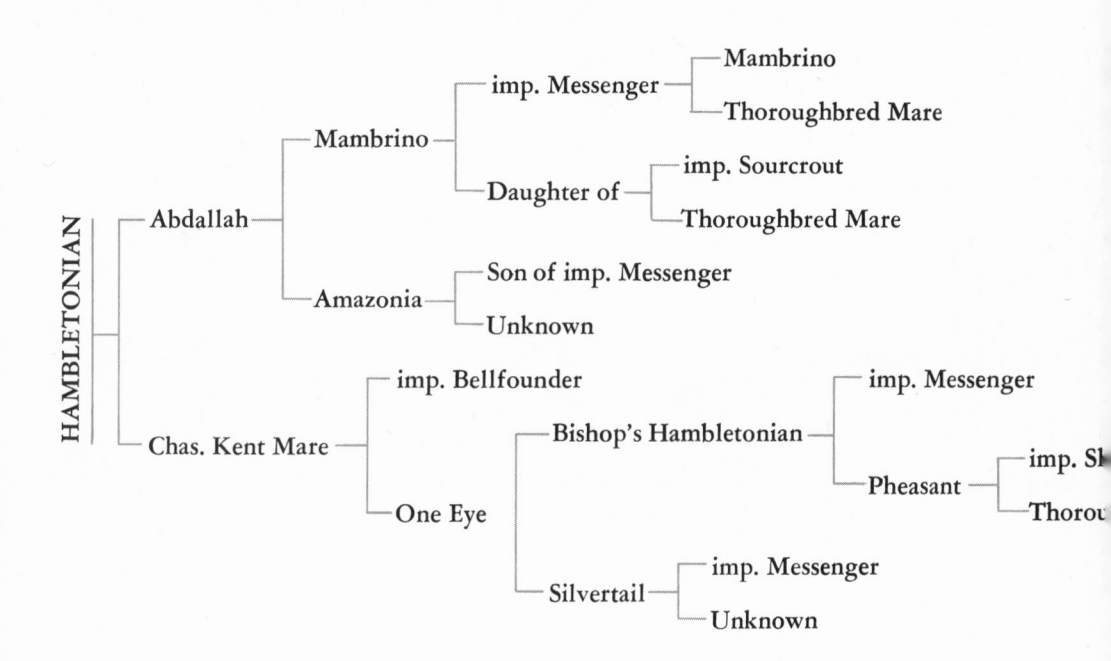

AMERICAN AS RED, WHITE AND BLUE

Hambletonian sired a record 1,330 foals. Many became road horses and were never raced, except in neighborly brushes. Many were not registered. But of those that were, forty trotted the mile in 2:30 or less, and 230 became sires or dams of speed.

An early son of Hambletonian, George Wilkes, fathered ninety-four foals. His twenty-three most notable offspring produced 200 notable sons and daughters. Add to these the tribes of Adballah 15, Volunteer, Dictator, Happy Medium, Harold, Strathmore, Electioneer, Artillery, Fleetwing and a galaxy of others and the sheer power of the Hambletonian family becomes apparent.

Titan Hanover, the first two-year-old to trot a two-minute mile, 1944

The United States Trotting Association estimates that 90% of the 430,374 registered Standardbreds can be traced straight back to Hambletonian through at least one line; or sometimes, as was the case with Titan Hanover, through eight crosses.

Hambletonian's greatest monument and triumph is the world's premier trotting classic, the Hambletonian. This futurity for three-year-olds is held each August at the State Fair Grounds in Du Quoin, Illinois. With affection more than disrespect sportswriters often call it the Hayseed Derby because of the homespun flavor of the agricultural fair. The drivers are sometimes 180-pound, white-haired owners or trainers who cluck their horses home to take two heats* out of three.

* A "heat" is one time around the one-mile track.

Nevele Pride esablished the new world record in 1969 with a blazing 1:54¼

This double—sometimes triple—test calls for greater stamina than is required of the Thoroughbred. It also demands great control, for the Standardbred must hold to the trotting gait instead of breaking into a wild gallop.

Thoroughbred racing may be the sport of kings, but harness racing belongs to the American people. The Hambletonian Stake is becoming so popular that in 1977 the total purse amounted to $270,000 while the purse for the Kentucky Derby was $267,000.

Hayseed Derby, indeed!

More than a century has passed since the time of Hambletonian 10, but the dynasty which he founded has spread far beyond Orange County, New York, to Australia and every other foreign country where harness speed is valued. Even the Russian Orloff breed of trotters was transformed by Hambletonian blood.

While it took three foundation sires—the Godolphin Arabian, Darley's Arabian, and Byerly Turk—to establish the Thoroughbred,

Hambletonian alone founded the Standardbred. His breed is democratically American; performance, not lineage, is the standard.

It wasn't that Hambletonian had no competition. There were other fine families—the Stars, the Pilots, the Blue Bulls—to challenge him, but his blood submerged them all so that today he reigns supreme.

As William Rysdyk might have said, and probably did, *"Never was anything like him."*

Hambletonian 10, as a three-year-old in 1852, driven by William Rysdyk

PAINTING BY GEORGE FORD MORRIS

BOOKS CONSULTED

Akers, Dwight, *Drivers Up!*

Bascom, Frederick G., *Letters of a Ticonderoga Farmer, 1851–1885*

Bloomfield, Leonard, *Colloquial Dutch*

Bostwick, Dunbar, *The Sport of Harness Racing*

Brooks, Van Wyck, *The World of Washington Irving*

Busbey, Hamilton, *Recollections of Men and Horses*

Chamberlain, George Agnew, *Overcoat Meeting*

Cloete, Stuart, *The Turning Wheels*

Crevecoeur, J. Hector St. John, *Letters From an American Farmer*

Dulles, Foster Rhea, *America Learns to Play*

Denhardt, Robert Moorman, *The Horse of the Americas*

De Voe, Thomas F., *Market Book, Containing a historical account of the public markets in the cities of New York, Boston, Philadelphia, and Brooklyn*

Gay, Carl W., *Productive Horse Husbandry*

Geers, Ed, *Ed Geers' Experience With the Trotters and Pacers*

Gocher, W. H., *Fasig's Tales of the Turf*

Gocher, W. H., *Trotalong*

Gocher, W. H., *Racealong*

Herbert, Henry William, *Frank Forester's Horse and Horsemanship of the United States and British Provinces of North America*

Hervey, John, *Messenger*

Hervey, John, *The American Trotter*

Johnstone, J. H. S., *The Horse Book, A practical treatise on the American horse breeeding industry as allied to the farm*

Krout, John Allen, *Pageant of America: Annals of American Sport*

Levy, S. J., *Chester, N.Y.: A History*

Mosre, P. W., *Greyhound*

Muybridge, E. J., and Stillman, J. D., *The Horse in Motion*

New York, A Guide to the Empire State

O'Hare, John Richard, *Socioeconomic Aspects of Horse Racing*

Partridge, Bellamy, and Bettman, Otto, *As We Were: Family Life in America 1850–1900*

Peters, Harry T., *Currier and Ives: Printmakers to the American People*

Rawson, Marion Nicholl, *Forever the Farm*

Sharts, Elizabeth, *Cradle of the Trotter*

Splan, John, *Life With the Trotters, With a chapter on how Goldsmith Maid and Dexter were trained (from information furnished by Mr. Budd Doble)*

Stephens, Henry, *The Book of the Farm*

Stong, Phil, *Horses and Americans*

Sullivan, George, *Harness Racing*

Thomas, Gertrude I., *Food of Our Forefathers*

Underwood, Tom R., editor, *Thoroughbred Racing and Breeding*

United States Trotting Association 1977 Year Book

Wallace, John H., *Trotting Register*

Woodruff, Hiram, *The Trotting Horse of America: How to Train and Drive Him, With reminiscences of the trotting turf*

Wrensch, Frank A., *Harness Horse Racing in the United States and Canada*